JANE AUSTEN

An Illustrated Treasury

JANE AUSTEN

An Illustrated Treasury

Rebecca Dickson

METRO BOOKS
NEW YORK

© 2008 by becker&mayer! Books

This 2008 edition published by Metro Books.

Design: Paul Barrett and Todd Bates
Editorial: Kjersti Egerdahl
Image Research: Chris Campbell
Production Coordination: Leah Finger

Metro Books
122 Fifth Avenue
New York, NY 10011

ISBN-13: 978-1-4351-0468-6
ISBN-10: 1-4351-0468-4

Printed in China through Legend Color Ltd., Hong Kong

10 9 8 7 6 5 4 3 2 1

Contents

Introduction

JANE AUSTEN

It is a truth universally acknowledged that every generation must rediscover Jane Austen.

Millions of women lived in the English-speaking

world of 1811, and a very few of them were famous, but not the author of a novel published that year called *Sense and Sensibility*. Though critics and readers liked the book, they knew only that it had been written "by a lady."

Today, by some fortunate twists of fate, the anonymous author of *Sense and Sensibility* has become one of the most popular writers in the world. Jane Austen's name is as recognizable as the nineteenth century's Queen Victoria and the sixteenth century's Queen Elizabeth I.

Love of Austen's works appears to be growing, not diminishing, in the new millennium. Who else has had five new television productions made based on her books and two recent major films based on her life and influence? And that's just the screen adaptations in 2006 and 2007. Dozens of film and TV productions based on Jane Austen's life and works have appeared since the 1930s. Jane Austen is a phenomenon—readers and viewers simply cannot get

To find out how popular Jane Austen is with young people today, I asked two college classes made up exclusively of first-year students fresh out of high school to name an Englishwoman who lived before 1850. One class named Queen Victoria, Elizabeth I, and Jane Austen. Another class named Queen Victoria, Jane Austen, and Joan of Arc (oops).

Portrait of Jane Austen, based on the sketch by her sister Cassandra, circa 1873.

enough of her. And literary critics have certainly never stopped writing books about her. Proof of Austen's appeal goes beyond books and films, though: one wonders what Austen would say if she knew an action figure has been made to look like her—once someone carefully explained to her what an action figure is.

Yet Jane Austen did not seek out fame. She published anonymously, so no direct acclaim could arise from her books. She did not mix with the famous authors of her day, so no notice would come through affiliation. Though she took pride in having her books published and she clearly loved to write, the publication of her books brought her only a little extra money and personal satisfaction; being a published author did not drastically change her lifestyle. A stranger passing Miss Austen on the street would have no reason to believe he was looking at the woman who, some two hundred years later, would represent their era.

Miss Austen's appeal

Jane Austen wouldn't understand our fascination with her, as our world appears to have so little in

I am a co-owner of a Jane Austen action figure. My book group, which sprouted because of our love of Jane Austen, owns one. Whoever volunteers to host the next meeting, at which we consume copious amounts of chocolate and wine, gets to take home the Jane action figure.

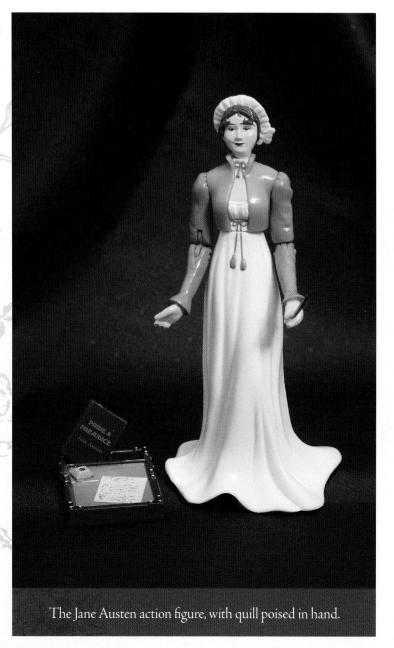

The Jane Austen action figure, with quill poised in hand.

common with hers. Largely gone are the bucolic country scenes she knew and loved, the scenes that she offers glimpses of in her novels. Servants no longer deliver notes or letters—actual paper missives seem rather quaint today. Automobiles, world wars, trips to the moon, cures for diseases—that a world this detached from hers could so adore her would have bewildered Jane Austen, to say nothing of her shock that we all appear to be wearing merely our underwear as we walk the streets of our cities. Yet today people of all backgrounds read Austen: ultrasound technicians, hospital administrators, magazine editors, software designers, computer programmers, photographers, English and math teachers, and travel agents (i.e., my book group).

> *So why this phenomenon known as Jane Austen?*
> *This woman who was not rich, not beautiful,*
> *whose name was not attached to her books*
> *while she was alive—why is she remembered?*

There's no full answer to this. Any great writer's work possesses a mystique that defies easy categorization, and that certainly applies to Jane Austen. But there are a few obvious reasons for her appeal. Austen draws readers in part because she provides an antidote to our modern world. In our fast-paced lives, the slower routine of carriages, walks, and afternoon teas has great appeal. Her genre explains her popularity as well: she wrote romantic comedies with relatable characters, and these will always find readers. Austen also pegged certain human traits accurately and amusingly, without mercy at some times and tenderly at others. She

With her insight about the human heart and the female mind, Jane Austen becomes a private best friend to many of her readers.

understood essential human relationships, and those haven't changed that much. By turns people can still be greedy and selfish, generous and compassionate, and always will be. Austen understood this.

With her insight about the human heart and the female mind, Jane Austen becomes a private best friend to many of her readers. Her novels give readers diary-like glimpses into the lives of troubled heroines; she sympathizes with her heroines, which has convinced many Austen readers that she would sympathize with them as well. Austen achieves this primarily through her characterizations: her protagonists are likeable

The Rules of Inheritance

PRIMOGENITURE, THE traditional inheritance system in Britain during Jane Austen's life, limited the financial possibilities of everyone but first-born sons: it dictated that the oldest son would inherit the bulk of an estate and the title. This was a tradition based on ancient law that the British would follow through Austen's lifetime and into the Victorian era. Primogeniture existed in part because of the fear that if an estate were divided up equally between all one's children, Britain's wealth would be decentralized and properties broken up. So to preserve properties mostly intact, usually second and third and other younger sons of landowning fathers went into the military, the clergy, or the law to provide for themselves and their families. Fathers often set aside seed money for their younger sons to move into such positions.

Fathers of means also usually set aside money for their daughters' husbands to receive upon their marriage, known as dowries. Women without wealthy fathers were simply unfortunate. If a woman was beautiful and accomplished, a well-to-do man might notice and marry her even though she had no money. Beauty, then, became a tool.

English men and women of the gentry class had little freedom to improve their lot—they could not pursue a career or open a business for fear of marking themselves as *needing* to work and therefore having a lower social standing. Both men and women needed to receive their wealth, not earn it. A woman's ability to maintain or improve her position largely depended on the men around her— her father, brothers, and husband. If a husband did not materialize, a gentry woman would become a "spinster" and, to some degree, a burden on her family.

But gentry women did not suffer the most in Britain, not by any means; they had enough food to eat and a roof over their heads. Those most badly served by Britain's hierarchy were the laboring classes, the majority of the population. For them, the British system was a caste system that left them few choices.

In a way, though, Britain's class system served nearly everyone poorly. While Austen was alive, British citizens of all economic levels continually measured themselves, their incomes, and their prospects against their neighbors. At best, this had to be fatiguing.

but fallible young women caught in situations that the reader can recognize.

Austen's plots are clever but simple enough to remain believable and realistic. In all of her books, she writes of situations and characters she knows and can portray with accuracy and wit: sisters with poor prospects for the future, lucky young men adopted into rich households, sea captains returning home after roaming the world. And her romances tracing how a couple becomes a couple—of eternal interest to readers—are wise and entertaining and deftly presented. Austen's books have a core of common sense, and her main characters, however flawed, have a captivating likeability that explains some of their wide appeal.

This approach to a protagonist still sells well— consider the popularity of Helen Fielding's 1996 novel *Bridget Jones's Diary*. Fielding creates deliberate parallels between Bridget Jones and Elizabeth Bennet of *Pride and Prejudice*, and Mark Darcy has much in common with his namesake, Fitzwilliam Darcy. It's no accident that the 2001 film version casts Colin Firth as Mark Darcy— Firth played the most memorable Fitzwilliam Darcy yet in the BBC's 1995 adaptation of *Pride and Prejudice*.

The novelist becomes an artist

This anonymous author also opened up a door into a new art form in her own time; the respected critic F. R. Leavis declared in 1948 that Jane Austen was "the inaugurator of the great tradition of the English novel." He asserts that she transformed the possibilities of the novel, both for novelists and readers, and this she did. Though novels became more acceptable in the 1700s, many writers and readers still considered them a lesser literary form than verse. The most admired writers of Austen's era wrote poetry: think William Cowper, William Wordsworth, Lord Byron, John Keats. The fact that novels didn't get as much respect as poetry made it easier for women to try writing them. Austen was one of the first to establish her own style and explore different possibilities of this relatively new form of writing. She created a new breed of woman on the written page.

> *Neither angel nor whore nor passive flower, as many heroines were before Austen's novels, her heroines are self-aware women, or become that way; they make mistakes, recognize them, and address them.*

A number of Austen's novels—*Sense and Sensibility*, *Pride and Prejudice*, and *Persuasion*—also can be read as subtle protests against a class and inheritance system that was coldly unfair to any non-firstborn child, especially if that child was female.

Underestimating Austen

Jane Austen's innovations and social criticisms don't appeal to some readers, though, in part because a faulty reputation precedes her. Starting in the mid-nineteenth century, Austen became the favorite of many readers and critics who presented her as a proper writer of moral tales, a delicate spinster who presented a tidy and lovely world—in

The fact that novels didn't get as much respect as poetry made it easier for women to try writing them.

their literary hands, Austen became merely a writer of the sweet romance where everything turns out well. Damage done. As a result of these "gentle Janeites," a term coined in the Victorian era, some readers loathe Jane Austen. Mark Twain is one of the most famous anti-Janeites. In a 1909 letter to writer William Dean Howells, he criticizes Edgar Allan Poe's writing, then says this of Jane Austen:

Mother–Daughter Tensions

EIGHTEENTH-CENTURY gentry families often sent their infants to a wet nurse soon after birth, and the Austen family did this with all of their children, including Jane. She lived with a wet nurse nearby for a year or so, only returning to her family when she didn't require the amount of time that an infant does. The Austen biographer Claire Tomalin points out that it was probably wrenching to young Jane to leave her mother and wonders if this early separation contributed to a lifelong coolness between mother and daughter. Mrs. Austen appears not to have understood her youngest daughter and to have preferred Cassandra. The years did not improve matters. Tomalin tells us that Mrs. Austen welcomed having a new daughter-in-law when her son James married; by then her children were adults. In 1797 Mrs. Austen wrote rather dismissively of Jane to the new daughter: "I look forward to you as a real comfort to me in my old age, when Cassandra is gone into Shropshire, & Jane—the Lord knows where." No one can know today what Austen's relationship with her mother was. But it is compelling to note that Austen portrayed the mothers in her books as silly, ineffectual, hysterical, absent, vain, or just plain dead.

Left: Silhouette of Jane Austen, based on an earlier silhouette thought to depict Jane Austen. Right: Silhouette of Jane's mother, Mrs. George Austen, born Cassandra Leigh.

"To me [Poe's] prose is unreadable—like Jane Austin's [*sic*]. No, there is a difference. I could read his prose on salary, but not Jane's. Jane is entirely impossible. It seems a great pity that they allowed her to die a natural death."

But Austen's talent has withstood the efforts of the Janeites, the anti-Janeites, and their modern counterparts. Most literary critics respect Austen immensely and see her as a key figure in literature.

Whether a critic approves of Austen or not, all have to agree that Austen has considerably influenced the writers who followed her, including George Eliot, Henry James, Charles Dickens, and many others.

In 1847, critic G. H. Lewes called Jane Austen the "prose Shakespeare" of the early nineteenth century. Shakespeare's plays lend themselves to many different interpretations and appeal to audiences from the illiterate to the highly learned. Austen has managed quietly to do the same thing, sans the iambic pentameter. Given that the world doesn't read as much poetry anymore, and prose is no longer considered a lesser art, Austen's amusing romances were bound to snowball into broad appeal.

Every summer at playhouses and outdoor theaters all across the English-speaking world, Shakespeare is rediscovered. And via films and TV series and play productions and newly published editions of her works, via biographies and articles and essays, via paper dolls, finger puppets, action figures and doggy t-shirts, so is Jane Austen.

A brief biography

Jane Austen was born on December 16th, 1775, the seventh child of eight children. Her father, George Austen, was a well-educated clergyman; her mother, Cassandra Leigh Austen, came from an old English family. The Austens belonged to the gentry class, barely; they did not have much money. Young Jane had six brothers and one sister, Cassandra. This large family lived in the rectory at Steventon, a village in Hampshire some fifty miles southwest of London. The rectory had a small farm attached to it, with a dairy and chicken coop. Though the family had servants to help run the house and farm, the Austen children helped with chores around the household.

The Austen home in Jane's youth was active and fun, with plenty of people around to keep things interesting. Her father, not a rich man but an intelligent one, opened the home to young male boarders whom he tutored, making the house all the more lively. The large library at the parsonage offered many diversions; the family read aloud to each other,

Jane's childhood home, Steventon Rectory. Drawing by her niece, Anna Lefroy, circa 1820.

The Sisters, by James W. Usher, circa 1880. Throughout her life, Jane's closest bond was with her sister Cassandra.

and when the Austen boys were older, they began putting on plays at home, which young Jane enjoyed very much.

Jane Austen's relationship with her older sister Cassandra was the most important one of her life. They grew up as the only girls surrounded by brothers and male boarders, which strengthened their bond all the more. The two sisters went away to boarding school together when Jane was seven and Cassandra ten. They stayed with a widow who housed and tutored the girls first at Oxford and later at Southampton. In that port town, the girls became very ill with a fever, and seven-year old Jane nearly died. The two girls returned home to recover, and a year or so later they were sent together to Reading for more education. They lived there for more than a year, then returned home for good. While at school, Jane and Cassandra would have studied history and geography; they also would have read literature deemed appropriate for girls and learned the basics of dancing, drawing, languages, music, and painting. When the girls returned home, their parents would have supervised them as they continued to study such topics, but they received no other formal education.

Not long after finally returning to Steventon, Jane Austen began writing for her family, and they supported her efforts, listening as she read her works aloud. At age eleven she wrote her first pieces of the *Juvenilia;* she wrote the last item of her *Juvenilia* when she was seventeen. She began writing *Elinor and Marianne,* the first version of *Sense and Sensibility,* a few years later, probably at nineteen. And she began writing *First Impressions*, the early draft of *Pride and Prejudice*, in 1796, when she was twenty years old.

Coming of age

By 1796, Jane Austen was an adult, a young woman who could marry. So as daughters of a traditional gentry family, Jane and Cassandra and other young women of the area attended balls and social events with an eye to finding a suitable young man, preferably one with plenty of money attached to him. Austen would not have been the most beautiful woman in the room at these events, nor would she have been the plainest. In the one surviving sketch that was made of Austen's face while she was alive—drawn by her sister Cassandra— we see a woman with a small mouth, a small nose, and large eyes. Dark curls encircle her face; her hair is tucked into a kerchief. Her mouth is set in a firm line, suggesting determination and strong character. Members of Austen's family claimed that the sketch did not do Austen justice; as Austen scholar Deirdre Le Faye reports, Austen's niece Anna Lefroy considered the drawing "hideously unlike" her aunt Jane.

Austen received at least one marriage proposal, which she refused because she did not love her suitor; she also likely had more than one romantic interlude in her life. But she never married, and lived most of her adult life with her mother and Cassandra, who

also remained single. (Cassandra's fiancé died before they could marry.) That Austen didn't marry made all the difference to her writing. Had she become a wife in that world with little birth control, she would have probably soon been pregnant. As a wife and mother, her home, children, and husband would have taken all

Jane Austen's relationship with her older sister Cassandra was the most important one of her life.

her time. She would have almost certainly been forced to leave her youthful ambition to write behind her.

Men could be writers in the nineteenth century, whatever their marital status; Walter Scott and Charles Dickens, for instance, both married and had many children. But single women of Austen's era faced many obstacles as they tried to write, and wives and mothers found it nearly impossible to do so.

Painting of cottage and church in Chawton, on Edward Austen-Leigh's estate of Godmersham, 1809.

When Austen was twenty-five, her father retired and moved to the famous resort town of Bath with his wife and daughters. Bath had many attractions, but it also had a reputation as a place for young people to find spouses, which is likely one reason that Mr. and Mrs. Austen chose to move there. Mr. Austen died in Bath in 1805, when Austen was twenty-nine, which caused great emotional and financial hardship for the women in his life. Mrs. Austen and her two daughters moved to smaller, less expensive lodgings, along with an unmarried family friend, Martha Lloyd. In 1807, the Austens moved to the port city of Southampton, and in 1809, they moved to a village back in Hampshire called Chawton, where they lived in a cottage owned by Austen's brother Edward.

Throughout these travels and moves and losses, Austen apparently wrote very little—whether she was depressed or just busy is open to speculation. Once settled permanently in Chawton, though, she began working on *Sense and Sensibility* again; the book was published in 1811. She then revised *First Impressions* into *Pride and Prejudice*, which appeared in January 1813. In the remaining years of her life, Austen wrote *Mansfield Park*, *Emma*, and *Persuasion*. She also began several other works and lightly revised *Northanger Abbey*. She likely expected to continue her prolific and successful writing, but she died in July 1817 at age 41, probably of Addison's disease.

Polishing the author's image

After her death, Austen's family depicted her as a quiet, docile, religious spinster. Henry Austen, her favorite brother and her agent of sorts, introduced her to the world after her death with the combined

Throughout these travels and moves and losses, Austen apparently wrote very little—whether she was depressed or just busy is open to speculation.

publication of *Northanger Abbey* and *Persuasion*; for the first time, the volumes were published under her name. Henry says this of his sister's appearance in the "Biographical Notice of the Author" he published with her books: "Her complexion was of the finest texture. It might with truth be said, that her eloquent blood spoke through her modest cheek. Her voice was extremely sweet." He goes on to say this of her personality: "Faultless herself, as nearly as human nature can be, she always sought, in the faults of others, something to excuse, to forgive or forget. . . . She never uttered either a hasty, a silly, or a severe expression. In short, her temper was as polished as

her wit." Even that isn't enough; several pages later, Henry comments on her piety: "She was thoroughly religious and devout; fearful of giving offence to God, and incapable of feeling it towards any fellow creature. On serious subjects she was well-instructed, both by reading and meditation, and her opinions accorded strictly with those of our Established Church." Though this description sounds rather cloying to twenty-first-century readers, it would have been quite a compliment for a woman in 1818.

Cassandra helped to obscure anything improper in Jane Austen's personality by destroying many of her letters and private papers after she died; if any indelicate opinions existed there, they are long gone. Austen's niece Fanny also destroyed many letters written by Austen. They didn't do this out of malice—many women of the era asked to have their writings and private effects burned after their death. Given the close scrutiny that English culture devoted to proper female behavior, Cassandra's destruction of her sister's more private thoughts is understandable.

The woman behind the words

To some degree, Jane Austen's published words contradict her family's efforts to present her as a delicate early nineteenth-century woman. There is a more complex woman behind these books. Austen

Left: Portrait of Jane's father, George Austen. Right: Her brother Henry, in his curate's attire.

clearly paid careful attention to relationships. She studied human nature, noted interactions between people, and recorded their foibles and strengths. Her family's loving description of her notwithstanding, the person who produced book after book about women who were economically and socially without choices, about clergymen who were silly fops, about powerful, rich characters who were often monstrous—this person could not have thought that all was perfect in her world. She understood that the British socioeconomic system made women entirely dependent on men, leaving them with little opportunity to improve their lives.

> *Austen knew that success often owes more to inheritance and connections than to personal merit and ability; she noticed the domineering gentlemen and ladies who did nothing to deserve their privileged positions, and she noticed the kind and deserving people who did nothing to deserve their difficult fates. Such characters people all her novels.*

Jane Austen's widespread popularity today proves her mighty talent and reflects the multifaceted books she wrote, in which she connects with many of her readers in a way that few other writers have

matched—and this across a span of two hundred years. As the decades pass and our culture changes, we read Austen differently; each generation re-interprets her in the context of their own era's expectations. The films based on Austen's novels and the critical responses to each book make clear

Given the close scrutiny that English culture devoted to proper female behavior, Cassandra's destruction of her sister's more private thoughts is understandable.

how much a reader's perspective on Austen depends on that reader's culture. But it's intriguing that, at their center, new interpretations of Austen's works remain loyal to her vision of the world, to her wise and unblinking recognition of the wrong, silly, or fine aspects of human nature. This timelessness in Austen has led to an ongoing curiosity about her. With snippets and snapshots of Austen's life and times and discussion of her art, we'll explore why Austen is one of the most popular and important writers who ever lived. We'll try once again to satisfy that unquenchable curiosity about this woman so many claim as their own literary best friend.

JANE AUSTEN'S EARLIEST WRITINGS:
THE JUVENILIA

Between the ages of eleven and seventeen, Jane Austen wrote a collection of short pieces known as the *Juvenilia*. Some of the sketches are very brief—a paragraph long—and others run up to fifty pages or more. These are Austen's least-read works, primarily because they were started by a child and finished by a teenager. Despite their unpolished form, any reader who knows Austen's works will recognize the *Juvenilia* as an expression of the developing writer. It's not an expression her family appreciated, though; the *Juvenilia* were not collected and published until more than a hundred years after Austen's death. Her family considered the early sketches indelicate, and by their standards in 1817, when Austen died, they were right. But the *Juvenilia* can also make a reader laugh out loud in places.

Austen's family situation partly explains the indelicacy. She had six brothers, five of whom were older, and her parents often kept male boarders, students whom Mr. Austen tutored. So Austen grew up in the open and boisterous atmosphere of boys. The *Juvenilia* smack of boys' influence at times, as in this creatively capitalized excerpt from "Memoirs of Mr. Clifford":

> *Mr. Clifford lived at Bath; & having never seen London, set off one monday morning determined to feast his eyes with a sight of that great Metropolis. He travelled in his Coach & Four, for he was a very rich young Man & kept a great many Carriages of which I do not recollect half. I can only remember that he had a Coach, a Chariot, a Chaise, a Landeau, a Landeaulet, a Phaeton, a Gig, a Whisky, an italian Chair, a Buggy, a Curricle & a wheelbarrow.*

The narrator's preoccupation with vehicles demonstrates the influence of older brothers who likely rattled on and on about them—as males of the species often do. Back then it was coaches, chaises, and horses; today it's sports cars, SUVs, and horsepower. One can visualize a room full of boys howling with laughter over her list of various vehicles that ends on the word "wheelbarrow."

Throughout "Jack and Alice," another "novel," Austen demonstrates her love of humor and satire. The character Lady Williams describes our heroine, Alice, in this way:

"'She has many rare & charming qualities, but Sobriety is not one of them. The whole Family are indeed a sad

drunken set. I am sorry to say too that I never knew three such thorough Gamesters [gamblers] as they are, more particularly Alice. But she is a charming girl . . .'" Unexpected events unfold in the tale: A lady sets a leg bone and instantaneously heals the wounded woman, a duke marries a young woman raised in a pub, a young gentlewoman murders another woman and is hanged. Alcohol flows freely, and love is won and lost easily. The indelicacy here will disappear in Austen's more mature works, but not the playfulness.

"The Three Sisters" is another piece worth reading, as it contains elements that Austen returns to. It is an epistolary story, consisting entirely of letters from one character to another, which Austen would try in *Elinor and Marianne*, the first version of *Sense and Sensibility*. In the first letter, young Mary Stanhope writes to a friend about the man who's recently proposed to her. Mary repeatedly says she hates him, but she wants what he can give her: a carriage, a nice home, higher status among the neighbors. Foreshadowing of Charlotte Lucas of *Pride and Prejudice*? Or Maria Rushworth of *Mansfield Park*? They both marry with eyes wide open, fully aware that their husbands are odious but needing to connect themselves to well-off men.

When the suitor arrives to ask Mary for her answer, the conversation seems familiar: "'Well Miss Stanhope I hope you have *at last* settled the Matter in your own mind; & will be so good as to let me know whether you will *condescend* to marry me or not.'" Mary answers in a way any reader of *Pride and Prejudice* recognizes: "'I think

Sir (said Mary) You might have asked in a genteeler way than that.'" The lines read like an early draft of the exchange between Mr. Darcy and Elizabeth during his first proposal.

Mary accepts her suitor's proposal, though she still hates him, and then she meets a handsome male

> *Even as a girl, Austen recognized that marriage was one of her society's fundamentals—yet she poked fun at it nonetheless.*

newcomer whom the three sisters all like. Mary again appears to be an early sketch of Maria Bertram, who gets into the same predicament in *Mansfield Park*.

Even as a girl, Austen recognized that marriage was one of her society's fundamentals—yet she poked fun at it nonetheless. One of her young female characters declares the following: "I expect my Husband to be good tempered and Chearful; to consult my Happiness in all his Actions, & to love me with Constancy & Sincerity." Her suitor stares at her, saying, "'These are very odd Ideas truly young lady. You had better discard them before you marry, or you will be obliged to do it afterwards.'" Luckily, Jane Austen never gave up her "very odd Ideas" about love and life.

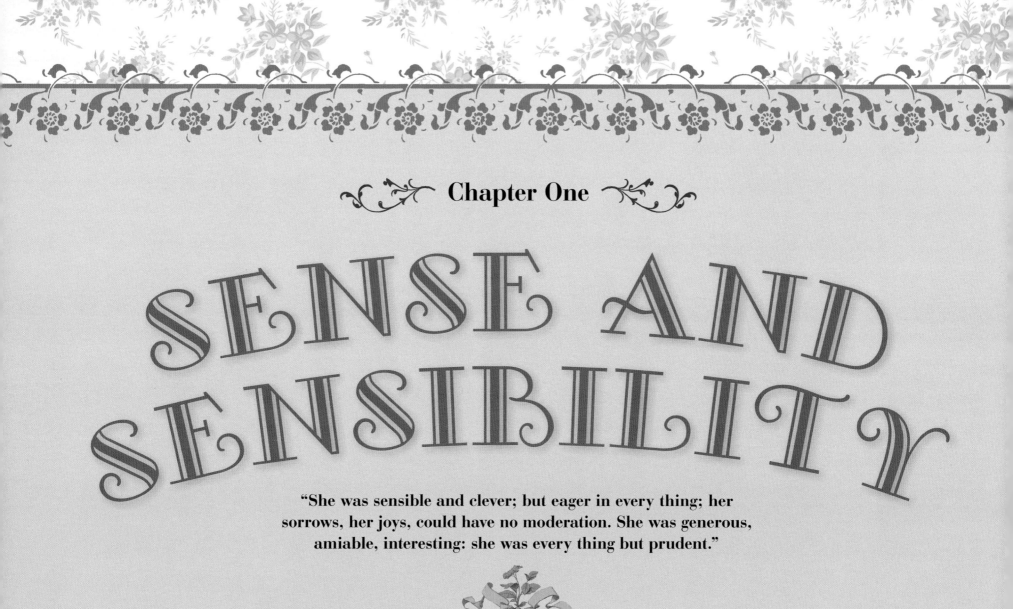

Chapter One

SENSE AND SENSIBILITY

"She was sensible and clever; but eager in every thing; her sorrows, her joys, could have no moderation. She was generous, amiable, interesting: she was every thing but prudent."

With the publication of her first book,

Sense and Sensibility, Jane Austen earned a real income for the first time in her life, at the age of thirty-six: she made 140 pounds, more than $8,000 in today's dollars. The novel appeared anonymously at the end of October in 1811, and sold out within two years. Given how often Austen writes of money and penniless women, and considering how dependent she was on her father's income and brothers' generosity—and how nervous she was about being discovered to be a writer—it must have been deeply satisfying to her to earn a substantial sum entirely on her own.

Sense and Sensibility had a long history before publication. In early 1795 Austen probably began writing the first draft, which she initially called *Elinor and Marianne*; she was still living at Steventon when she first set pen to paper. *Elinor and Marianne* no longer exists, but we know that it was an epistolary novel, that is, it was a series of letters various characters wrote to one another. This was a popular novel form during Austen's lifetime; eighteenth-century writer Samuel Richardson, one of her favorite authors, wrote both of his famous novels *Pamela* and *Clarissa* in this way.

After Austen finished that first draft, she set it aside and began writing another novel, the first version of *Pride and Prejudice*. In 1797 she revised *Elinor*

The Love Letter by Henry Le Jeune, 1871.

Photograph of the Austen family residence in Bath at No. 4 Sydney Place, circa 1920. The building has changed little since Jane lived here with her sister and parents in 1801–1804.

and Marianne, transforming it from the series of letters into *Sense and Sensibility*.

Austen's family moved to Bath in 1801, and her father died there in 1805. As far as we know, Austen wrote very little at Bath; as the biographer Claire Tomalin interprets the period, Austen went into a depression after leaving her beloved home at Steventon and moving to Bath, a town she did not like. So for a number of years, it appears that she was simply not writing. But in the summer of 1809, the widowed Mrs. Austen and her daughters Cassandra and Jane returned to Hampshire and moved into a cottage at Chawton. Back in her home county, Austen began writing again, and she revised the novel once more. By the winter of 1810, *Sense and Sensibility*, with its moving depiction of sisters weathering heartbreak and hard times, was accepted for publication.

The story of two sisters

Jane Austen is probably giving us a powerful bit of autobiography in the relationship between Elinor and Marianne, the heroines of *Sense and Sensibility*. Austen was certainly as close to her sister Cassandra as the sisters are in the novel. The Austen sisters grew up as the only girls in a houseful of boys and went off to school together when they were both very young. Cassandra, three years older than Jane, mothered her while away from home. Jane and her sister shared a bedroom for most of their lives and wrote to each other often when they were separated. After their father's death, they moved with their mother and family friend Martha Lloyd to a series of smaller homes; without the income from their father's clergyman position, the women of the family lived in near poverty.

The situation in *Sense and Sensibility* is also grim. Mr. Henry Dashwood dies early in the novel, and all his property goes to the son from his first marriage, John Dashwood, even though John Dashwood has a fine home already. The father asks his son to look after his second wife and his three daughters—the son's step-mother and half-sisters. The son means to do well, but his greedy, self-involved wife helps him to justify giving his relatives nothing. The Dashwood women—Mrs. Dashwood and her three teenage daughters, Elinor, Marianne, and Margaret—are pushed out of their home when Mr. and Mrs. John Dashwood arrive.

The Dashwood women move into a cottage in Devonshire, far away from their home, and start a new life. Marianne, an overly emotional seventeen-year-old, soon meets John Willoughby, a dashing young man who quickly wins her heart and gives her his—but without the security of a marriage proposal. Colonel Brandon, another neighbor, also falls in love with Marianne, but he's almost the opposite of Willoughby. He's not dashing, just steady and dependable—and he's thirty-five. He doesn't pursue Marianne because she makes it clear to everybody that she is madly in love with Willoughby.

Elinor is two years older than Marianne, and as pragmatic as Marianne is romantic. But she does fall quietly in love with Edward Ferrars, the brother of the nasty Mrs. John Dashwood. Edward is the opposite of his sister—he has a good heart. Edward loves Elinor back, but he is secretly engaged to Lucy Steele, a silly

Jane Austen is probably giving us a powerful bit of autobiography in the relationship between Elinor and Marianne, the heroines of Sense and Sensibility.

girl with a mean streak. Though he no longer loves Lucy, he doesn't feel he can end the engagement. He knows that women need to marry for their happiness and security, and he feels he can't abandon a frivolous and mean penniless woman for a kind and intelligent, equally penniless woman, no matter how much he loves Elinor.

Money troubles

The two sisters find themselves in an emotionally and financially vulnerable position; money is behind most of the conflict in the book. If they want to help their mother and young sister, they need to "marry well"—that is, each needs to become a rich man's wife. But because they have no money of their own to bring to a marriage, their chances of marrying well are slim. Austen knows this vulnerability from experience. She started writing *Sense and Sensibility* when she was about nineteen, at home in Steventon, but revised it in

The book is Austen's antidote to excessive emotion.

1809 after moving to a small house with the women of her family. Even as she watched her last chances at marriage slip away, she had to keep a careful eye on the family budget and resign herself to writing always in the sitting room.

In Austen's era, it was almost impossible for an unmarried woman to find a room of her own. This hard fact arose from Britain's laws concerning women and inheritance. One of the goals of male-only inheritance was to keep property intact, rather than split between several children—so it was realistic for Austen to depict a selfish half-brother inheriting every bit of property belonging to a father, and it was acceptable enough that

such a brother might not do anything to help support his half-sisters and stepmother.

Although Britain was a dominant world power, British gentry women had little control over their fates. Austen was aware of this fact, as she had no choice but to live with three other women without husbands for her entire adult life.

Marianne and Elinor also live with their widowed mother, and, if they do not marry, they too will live with their mother for the rest of their lives. But as *Sense and Sensibility* opens, the sisters are still young—there's hope for them.

"Maxims for the conduct of life"

It can be easy to forget how young Elinor and Marianne really are, but in truth, *Sense and Sensibility* is about two teenagers. Jane Austen wouldn't have understood that term, since in her time, the only recognized stages of life were childhood, adulthood, and old age; acknowledgement of the teen years wouldn't come for another century. But even though "teenagers" didn't exist socially for Austen, people between the ages of twelve and twenty have traits that were plain even then. Jane Austen, a teenager herself when she began the novel, wrote about teenagers and to some extent for teenagers. As such, *Sense and Sensibility* has some overt lessons in it for young women. But a story with lessons to teach is a tricky thing to write. They're completely out of style today. In the eighteenth and nineteenth centuries, though, many novel-readers expected to learn a lesson, so this could be a powerful form. Take Harriet Beecher Stowe's *Uncle Tom's Cabin*, a runaway bestseller in the United States that fueled the enthusiasm of the anti-slavery crowd before the Civil War. But that book isn't read much anymore, partly because of its dense moralizing.

Austen's *Sense and Sensibility*, however, continues to find readers, was adapted into a major film, and has recently been made into a new miniseries. Austen gets away with her overt lessons while other writers of the nineteenth century fade away, in part because she offers up her lessons differently than many of her fellow writers do. Austen does not teach with a heavy hand. Short chapters and witty descriptions keep the pace brisk, and the characters are likeable. But she writes with clear intent: she asks her teenage readers to look beyond appearances. Austen demonstrates to the impressionable Marianne Dashwood that the diffident Edwards, the somber Colonel Brandons, and the perfect Willoughbys of the world may have more or less to them than first appears. *Sense and Sensibility* advises readers to catch themselves before

reacting to a situation without thought; it also tells us not to brood over negative emotions. The book is Austen's antidote to excessive emotion.

In October 1811, when the novel first appeared, Austen's lessons met with general approval. A reviewer in the *British Critic* in May of 1812 advised female readers that *Sense and Sensibility* would be a worthwhile book: "They may peruse these volumes not only with satisfaction but with real benefits, for they may learn from them, if they please, many sober and salutary maxims for the conduct of life, exemplified in a very pleasing and entertaining narrative."

Marianne's flights of fancy

The book is certainly pleasing and entertaining, but it's not because Austen is particularly shy about her lessons—in *Sense and Sensibility*, she plainly presents Marianne as excessive and needing to change. But Austen not only laughs at Marianne, she laughs *with* Marianne, and that humor helps the reader see that excessive emotional display just feels, well, excessive, and there's not a lot of point to it, not after the initial relief.

Marianne takes herself seriously and she has serious emotions—and the Marianne we meet at the beginning of the book takes pride in this. It's also clear from this quotation how much of her era's romantic poetry she has been reading:

ENVELOPE CONTENTS

- *Selected pages from* one piece of Jane Austen's *Juvenilia*. At the age of sixteen, she wrote *The History of England*, a parody of Oliver Goldsmith's *History of England*, with illustrations by her sister Cassandra.

- *A letter from* Jane to Cassandra, in which she mentions correcting proofs of *Sense and Sensibility*.

Autumn by Frederick Walker, 1865.

" 'Dear, dear Norland!' said Marianne, as she wandered alone before the house, on the last evening of their being there: 'when shall I cease to regret you!—when learn to feel a home elsewhere!—Oh! happy house, could you know what I suffer in now viewing you from this spot, from whence perhaps I may view you no more!' "

Marianne indulges her intense emotions and shows no self-restraint in expressing them. A seventeen-year-old girl will usually face some knocks no matter what, but a seventeen-year-old who despises self-restraint is probably going to take a hard fall. And Marianne does. Her true love Willoughby leaves town suddenly—she doesn't find out the real reason until later, but he has gotten a girl pregnant, and his rich aunt responds by cutting him out of her will. A poor girl like Marianne doesn't seem so attractive after this, and he leaves the Dashwoods' neighborhood. Naturally, she is crushed when he's gone, although she doesn't know yet that it's over between them. Though sympathetic, Austen humorously describes Marianne's devotion to her own pain:

Marianne would have thought herself very inexcusable had she been able to sleep at all the first night after parting from Willoughby. She would have been ashamed to look her family in the face the next morning, had she not risen from her bed in more need of repose than when she lay down in it. But the feelings which made such composure a disgrace, left her in no danger of incurring it. She was awake the whole night, and she wept the greatest part of it. She got up with a headache, was unable to talk, and unwilling to take any nourishment; giving pain every moment to her mother and sisters, and forbidding all attempt at consolation from either. Her sensibility was potent enough!

Marianne spends the day after Willoughby leaves walking through Allenham, the site of Willoughby's estate, remembering all the places they used to walk together. Then in the evening she plays every song that she and Willoughby used to sing, and later looks through all the books they used to read together. With such passages, we have to laugh at Marianne. She is a teenager who is feeling great angst, certainly, but she's manufacturing at least part of it.

As Marianne's emotional excesses continue after Willoughby's exit, Elinor tries, again with humor, to get her younger sister to check herself. We see this when Edward trots back into the Dashwoods' world. Marianne learns that Edward has recently been at Norland and sees another opportunity to indulge her deep feelings.

"And how does dear, dear Norland look?" cried Marianne [to Edward].

Marianne & the Romantic Movement

MARIANNE DASHWOOD is a poster child for the Romantic era. Romantic poetry grew out of the Enlightenment but at the same time reacted against it; the movement protested the aristocracy, the class structure, and the dominance of scientific thought. Romanticism was all the rage during Austen's lifetime. It glorified nature and was profoundly nostalgic, elevating all things old and rustic—even dead leaves. When Marianne compares herself to a dead leaf in the midst of her melancholy thoughts on the absent Willoughby, she comes across as silly—but she also echoes the respected poets of her time. William Wordsworth, one of the key Romantic poets, was also a fan of forest litter. Consider what he says in this portion of his 1798 poem "A Whirl-Blast from Behind Hill."

> *Where leafless oaks towered high above,*
> *I sat within an undergrove*
> *Of tallest hollies, tall and green;*
> *A fairer bower was never seen.*
> *From year to year the spacious floor*
> *With withered leaves is covered o'er…*

Wordsworth goes on to express how the dead leaves skip and hop and dance in the wind. He even starts one of his sentences with "Oh!"—it was practically a Romantic tradition to do so, as Marianne often does.

We know that Austen read Romantic poetry. In her novels and letters, she refers to Robert Southey, Robert Burns, Walter Scott, and Wordsworth, all well-known Romantic writers. She also alludes to several poems by Lord Byron that he wrote in 1813 and 1814, but Austen likely read Byron's earlier work as well: Marianne personifies the Byronic hero. Byron's heroes tended to have a distaste for the social structure, and they were rebellious, throwing caution to the wind even if doing so resulted in self-destruction. They also embraced passion fiercely, preferring the emotional to the intellectual. And oh! how they loved nature. Remind you of anyone?

Clearly Austen has some fun with Marianne's character—but as usual in *Sense and Sensibility*, her humor comes with a lesson: she warns that taking the Romantic attitude too far can make one look a bit ridiculous, or worse.

Young Woman on her Death Bed by an anonymous member of the Flemish School, 1621.

Chapter One • *Sense and Sensibility*

"Dear, dear Norland," said Elinor, "probably looks much as it always does at this time of year. The woods and walks thickly covered with dead leaves."

"Oh!" cried Marianne, "with what transporting sensations have I formerly seen them fall! How have I delighted, as I walked, to see them driven in showers about me by the wind! What feelings have they, the season, the air altogether inspired! Now there is no one to regard them. They are seen only as a nuisance, swept hastily off, and driven as much as possible from the sight."

"It is not every one," said Elinor, "who has your passion for dead leaves."

The dry humor in that last line is unmistakable. Marianne is comparing herself to a dead leaf here, and Austen and Elinor want her to see how silly she is being.

On some level, Marianne's excesses are merely ridiculous, but they can lead to serious consequences. Austen warns her readers that indulging powerful emotions can have a price when she shows Marianne's reaction to Willoughby's final rejection of her: "This violent oppression of spirits continued the whole evening. [Marianne] was without any power, because she was without any desire of command over herself. The slightest mention of any thing relative to Willoughby overpowered her in an instant." Austen's use of the words "violent," "power," "command," and "overpowered" conveys a

warning: surrender to your pain and you surrender control over your circumstances. This can actually be dangerous: Marianne becomes violently ill, and nearly dies. Austen's admonitions against wallowing in powerful negative emotions still speak to us over the centuries.

What's also tucked in here is the burden that Marianne's self-indulgence puts on her family. Marianne's emotional outbursts deeply upset her

Austen warns her readers that indulging powerful emotions can have a price.

mother and sisters—and she doesn't care. They do everything they can think of to comfort her, and she shrugs them off like, well, a teenager. Marianne will not allow her concerned family to soothe her, and Austen presents this as selfish on her part.

Finding true love that lasts

Not caring about other people or social restrictions presents another form of danger, Austen asserts; in *Sense and Sensibility* she subtly asks her readers to consider the strong call of "love" at age seventeen versus the requirement in 1811 that a woman be chaste and virtuous. Much of such "love" is what we would call "hormones" today. Here Willoughby helps to deliver the lesson. His love affair with Eliza, and her resulting pregnancy, have cost him his inheritance—and Marianne, whom he genuinely loves.

Anyone who dismisses Austen as "sweet" should read her novels more carefully—they'll come across scorching passages relatively often.

Edward Ferrars, the nearly perfect match for the perfect Elinor, has a similar lesson to teach, for he also has let love mislead him: the young man who is so drawn to a pretty young woman that he forgets to consider other aspects of her personality may become a very unhappy man, unable to marry someone he really does love. Edward is unhappily trying to do the ethical thing by his "ignorant and illiterate" fiancée Lucy Steele. He made a commitment to her early on and he sees how she depends on him, but the more mature Edward knows he does not really love Lucy.

In case the reader somehow misses the lesson that Edward teaches here, Austen gives us Mr. and Mrs. Palmer, a desperately unhappy couple who married, again, because a young man was drawn by a pretty face. They may be the unhappiest couple in all of Austen's works, more poorly suited to one another even than Mr. and Mrs. Bennet of *Pride and Prejudice*. Mr. Palmer either entirely ignores his wife or harshly insults her, and whether others are present makes no difference whatsoever. That Mrs. Palmer almost deserves such treatment is beside the point; their inescapable marriage is Austen's lesson here. Austen shows how trapped they are in a startlingly harsh conversation between Mr. Palmer and his mother-in-law Mrs. Jennings. Mr. Palmer has just insulted Mrs. Jennings, which prompts Mrs. Palmer to speak up:

> "My love, you contradict every body," said his wife with her usual laugh, "Do you know that you are quite rude?"
>
> "I did not know I contradicted any body in calling your mother ill-bred."
>
> "Aye, you may abuse me as you please," said the good-natured old lady, "you have taken Charlotte off my hands, and cannot give her back again. So there I have the whip hand of you."

Mrs. Jennings wields the whip in this exchange: Mr. Palmer is indeed stuck with his Mrs. Palmer. In 1811, divorce was rare in England. It damaged a man's social reputation and destroyed a woman's, and it was difficult to achieve legally. But Mrs. Jennings's comment to her son-in-law is savage nonetheless, both to her daughter and him. Anyone who dismisses Austen as "sweet" should read her novels more carefully—they'll come across scorching passages such as this one relatively often.

> *Jane Austen's warning is clear: marry in haste, marry a handsome face without considering the rest of the package, and there is no way out.*

Austen's sympathetic side

Marianne does learn the lessons Austen puts before her. Late in the novel, she tells Elinor of her reflections while recovering from her illness, demonstrating that she knows she has acted excessively: "'I saw that my own feelings had prepared my sufferings, and that my want of fortitude under them had almost led me to the grave. My illness, I well knew, had been entirely brought on by myself, by such negligence of my own health, as I had felt even at the time to be wrong. Had I died,—it would have been self-destruction.'" Who knows how many seventeen-year-olds of Austen's era actually

Signing the Register by Edmund Blair Leighton (1853–1922). Austen's portrayals of marriage reflect its significance—and permanence—in her time.

The Waning Honeymoon by George Henry Boughton, 1878. Several of Jane Austen's characters, including Mr. and Mrs. Palmer, find themselves trapped in loveless marriages.

became this self-aware. But Marianne's clear-eyed appraisal of herself makes readers realize just how much she's learned.

Jane Austen doesn't simply sit in judgment of people with strong emotions, though. On the whole, she shows great sympathy for her characters.

> Sense and Sensibility *is one of Austen's warmest novels; she makes it clear that she does understand many of the inevitable problems that a young person faces while growing up.*

One of Austen's great achievements in the novel is the way she writes about first love. Her portrayal of Marianne and Willoughby speaks to any teenager in love. Marianne and Willoughby exist in perfect harmony with each other. They have the same taste in books, in music; they have the same views of life, the same feelings of rebellion against society's expectations of them. How many teenagers have fallen just as desperately in love? And how many have been just as betrayed by their lovers? It's become a common ritual for teenagers to love deeply and forever, and then face rejection.

Austen knew this and captures the pain of it all. When Elinor and Marianne attend a party in London, Marianne must suddenly acknowledge that Willoughby, her perfect man, really has abandoned her. She's written him numerous letters without getting a reply, yet still has hope—but then she sees him with a rich, fashionable young woman. Marianne broadcasts her reaction to Elinor: "'Good heavens!' she exclaimed, 'he is there—he is there—Oh! why does he not look at me? why cannot I speak to him?'" When Willoughby, who tries to ignore her, finally does approach them, she cannot repress her shock and anger and despair: "'Good God! Willoughby, what is the meaning of this? Have you not received my letters? Will you not shake hands with me?'" They talk uncomfortably for several minutes, then he returns to his fashionable lady, who has some fifty thousand pounds attached to her while Marianne has practically nothing. Marianne sinks into a chair: "'Go to him, Elinor,' she cried, as soon as she could speak, 'and force him to come to me. Tell him I must see him again—must speak to him instantly.—I cannot rest—I shall not have a moment's peace till this is explained—some dreadful misapprehension or other.—Oh go to him this moment.'"

Anyone who has suffered the loss of a first love aches while reading about Marianne's agony. The moment is not dramatized, and Marianne isn't manufacturing her pain this time. Austen simply shows what such a moment, in public, would be: a crushing, humiliating, infuriating blow.

Sense is Out of Style

THE 1995 FILM VERSION of *Sense and Sensibility* reflects the modern attitude toward Elinor, Austen's perfect heroine. Directed by Ang Lee and adapted by Emma Thompson, the film shows both Marianne and Elinor as needing to change, not just Marianne. In Austen's time, people recognized the danger of Marianne's heedlessness. The *British Critic* review of May 1812 makes this clear: "Not less excellent is the picture of the young lady of over exquisite sensibility, who falls immediately and violently in love with a male coquet, without listening to the judicious expostulations of her sensible sister, and believing it impossible for man to be fickle, false, and treacherous." There's nothing in the review about the lessons that Elinor must absorb, for in Austen's day, Marianne was the only sister who had something to learn.

We modern readers also get that Marianne is excessive. But our touchy-feely culture is convinced that concealing emotions is repressive, so Elinor has to let it all out. When Elinor discovers that Edward Ferrars is not married after all, she explodes with cathartic emotion. Today, this earns Emma Thompson an Oscar; Austen probably would have turned away from such a display.

An ideal sister

Elinor Dashwood, at nineteen, is the only real adult of the Dashwood women. She understands Marianne's trauma over losing Willoughby, but at the party where they encounter him, Elinor also realizes that Marianne will damage her reputation if she causes

Elinor is Austen's most fully drawn role model. In her, we see the author's idea of everything a proper woman should be.

a scene. So she does what she can to protect Marianne and call her back to reality while sympathizing with her sister's honest emotions. Their mother relies on Elinor nearly as much as Marianne does. Elinor does what her mother will not do: she watches their finances, she keeps herself and the family emotionally afloat during difficult times, she perseveres when Marianne becomes ill. She's also insightful, wise, and strong. Elinor is Austen's most fully drawn role model. In her, we see the author's idea of everything a proper woman should be.

Constantly thinking of others, Elinor does not emotionally collapse when Lucy Steele tells Elinor about her engagement to Edward Ferrars, the man Elinor loves, despite the hopelessness of her situation: "No one would have supposed from the appearance of the sisters, that Elinor was mourning in secret over obstacles which must divide her for ever from the object of her love." Elinor chooses not to tell her troubles to her mother and sisters, in part because she has promised Lucy Steele that she would not, but also because she does not want to communicate something that would be almost as painful to them as to her. She'd rather bear the burden alone.

Elinor is also capable of real compassion. After Willoughby's long story of woe in which he explains his behavior, "she forgave, pitied, wished him well—was even interested in his happiness." That she can still feel for Willoughby, the man who has so hurt her beloved sister, speaks highly of Austen's most morally strong protagonist.

Elinor tends to be unpopular with some modern readers, though, because she's too perfect. Austen's first readers would have had no problem reading about a flawless protagonist, because women of her time were expected to strive for pure, quiet perfection. The book's first reviews prove this by praising the lessons it teaches. But today the flawless woman seems impossible, even uninteresting. Our cool reception of Elinor reflects who we are as a culture: we are suspicious of a person who appears perfect and entirely self-contained.

Head and Shoulders of a Young Woman by Jean Baptiste Greuze, 18th century.

Marianne and Willoughby show their talents for intimate conversation in an illustration from an early edition of *Sense and Sensibility*, by Hugh Thompson, circa 1880.

Decorum and self-control seem hopelessly old-fashioned now. The more flawless a protagonist is, the more we look for cracks in her façade. We like antiheroes, or at least flawed characters we can root for, like Marianne—or Bridget Jones. We have rejected the perfect character just as we have rejected the novel with a moral.

The men in Marianne's life

Colonel Brandon is not a very popular character today, either, but he was also created as a role model. Though the brooding Alan Rickman drew some fans to Colonel Brandon in the 1995 film, Brandon is just not a winning sort of guy, which seems rather unfair. It's not his fault that he's thirty-five and past the first bubbly sensations of love. And should steadiness of character and commitment to others really be considered a character flaw? Alas, it is. Some readers see the coupling of Brandon and Marianne as Austen's betrayal of her seventeen-year-old protagonist.

Predictably enough, many readers like Willoughby, whom Austen meant to be a negative role model. Poor guy, he was just born in the wrong century. Willoughby would be totally accepted today. He'd be perpetually in credit-card debt, would borrow against his mortgage and refinance; he would get married and divorced early, saying "I do" at least three times before finding a fourth wife who could understand and accept his flakiness.

The connection between Edward Ferrars and Jane Austen's first love

Austen may have had a soft spot for the book's other male love interest, Edward Ferrars. Not only does she decide that he's worthy of her flawless Elinor, he's nearly as financially vulnerable as the two sisters, a rare thing for Austen's men. He also may have a few things in common with Austen's own first love, Tom Lefroy.

Edward is in a tight situation; he is relatively powerless over his future. Because of the way his family's inheritance works, Edward has to bow to the wishes of his mother, a faceless authority we see only briefly. She can change her will and make irrevocable decisions about others' lives with a stroke of her pen. Edward's mother has attempted to make him a public figure. He resists this, and his mother agrees to let him become a clergyman. His engagement to Lucy Steele is risky, because she has no money, and so he keeps it secret in part for fear of his mother's wrath. He is right to be cautious: when his mother discovers his engagement, she disinherits him.

Edward's situation resembles that of Austen's youthful crush Tom Lefroy, who had to "marry well" in order to inherit a solid income. Austen met Lefroy soon after her twentieth birthday; he was a law student from Ireland visiting family in the neighborhood. They danced at several balls together, and he called on her in her home at least once. Writing to Cassandra on January 9, 1796, Austen says that they talked of

books together, and it's clear that she is intrigued with Lefroy—possibly to the point of acting a little like Marianne, as her letter suggests:

> "You scold me so much in the nice long letter which I have this moment received from you, that I am almost afraid to tell you how my Irish friend and I behaved. Imagine to yourself everything most profligate and shocking in the way of dancing and sitting down together."

Edward's situation is similar to that of Austen's youthful crush Tom Lefroy, who had to "marry well" in order to inherit a solid income.

Jane's next letter to Cassandra shows her growing hopes of a future with Lefroy, but the hopes are mixed with flippant phrases, so it's difficult to discern how much Austen cared for him. In a letter to Cassandra of January 14–15, 1796, Austen looks forward to seeing Lefroy at the next ball, although she mocks his fashion sense: "I look forward

The Backlash Against Women Writers

ATTACHING HER NAME to her books would have been a risk for Jane Austen, since she was up against several cultural barriers. In 1811, published women writers often received negative attention, and few women looked forward to being publicly labeled as a woman with opinions. England was particularly conservative during Austen's lifetime because the French Revolution had begun tearing down the aristocracy in France in 1789. Seeing the chaos just across the English Channel, the powerful in England grew far less tolerant of new ideas at home.

In part, women writers were looked down upon on in the early 1800s because of the unconventional life of Mary Wollstonecraft. Today, she's celebrated as one of the first writers to push for women's rights: her most famous book, *A Vindication of the Rights of Woman*, argues that women only seemed inferior to men because they weren't offered the same quality of education. The book got positive reviews when it was first published in 1792, but Wollstonecraft's reputation was ruined when her husband William Godwin published his ac-

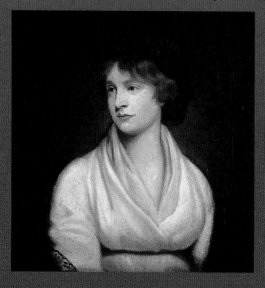

count of her life in 1798, after her death, and spoke openly of her affairs, illegitimate child, and suicide attempts. His book scandalized the reading public, and, as the English literary critic Marilyn Butler tells us, the publishing world became all the more wary of publishing literature by women. Feminist ideas became especially taboo for many years; Wollstonecraft's name would still have been infamous in 1811, when Austen's first novel was published.

Portrait of Mary Wollstonecraft by John Keenan, 1804.

with great impatience to it, as I rather expect to receive an offer from my friend in the course of the evening. I shall refuse him, however, unless he promises to give away his white Coat." The next day, January 15, Austen says this of meeting Lefroy: "At length the Day is come on which I am to flirt my last with Tom Lefroy, & when you receive this it will be over—My tears flow as I write, at the melancholy idea." Is she being ironic or serious? In the very next sentence, Austen goes on to discuss a neighbor who called, suggesting that no tears of any kind were flowing as she wrote of Lefroy's impending departure.

With the flippant phrases, Austen may have been protecting herself from hope for a marriage with Lefroy, for such a relationship wasn't likely. As Jon Spence tells us in his book *Becoming Jane Austen*, Lefroy was the eldest son of eleven children, and he had little money. In order to come into an inheritance from his great-uncle Benjamin Langlois, he needed to find a wealthy wife—and Jane Austen had no money.

Given that Austen revised *Elinor and Marianne* into *Sense and Sensibility* after she met Lefroy, it is possible she arranged her hero's fate to look much like Lefroy's: Edward also is caught in a mess, needing to do the practical thing but in love with a poor woman. The merciful Austen gives Edward more elbow room than Lefroy had—Edward does not have ten siblings hoping that he will do well financially so he can advance their interests as well. Edward's siblings already are well situated, so he can risk disinheritance. Lefroy could not.

The delicate subject of money

In spite of all the concern about money among Austen's class, it was unseemly to pursue it directly. Most jobs were taboo for men and women alike: ideally, money should be given to a person by someone else or "earned" by renting farmland to poorly paid members of the working classes.

The psychological tensions in the gentry mind of having so much power (over the working classes) and yet so much powerlessness (money must be received, not earned) pretty much made Sigmund Freud and psychoanalysis inevitable eighty years later.

Money was just as important in Austen's world as it is in ours, but women could almost never count on an inheritance, even one as uncertain as Edward's. And so Austen's women begin to think about income from a young age. In *Sense and Sensibility*, nineteen-year-old Elinor and seventeen-year-old Marianne discuss how much a young woman needs to survive. Marianne, who doesn't value money at all, declares she would need only two thousand pounds a year to be happy. Elinor laughs at this; she's the one who pays attention to the family budget, and she would

The Sisters by Margaret Sarah Carpenter (neé Geddes), circa 1839.

Photograph of Chawton centered on Jane Austen's home, taken circa 1920. The cottages at the left border the village pond, and the beginnings of the village center are visible at the right.

Chapter One • *Sense and Sensibility*

feel wealthy with one thousand pounds a year. What's most interesting here is that two teenage girls are thinking seriously about money and trying to define financial stability—while they themselves can do very little to achieve such security but look pretty and be accommodating to the young men they meet.

A writer against all odds

Jane Austen never achieved financial independence, and it was even difficult for her to achieve the independence of mind that a writer needs, given how little freedom women had to speak freely. At Chawton Cottage, the Austen women lived comfortably enough, but Austen still did not have a room of her own. She shared a bedroom with Cassandra, and had no dedicated place to write, so she wrote in the sitting room. As her nephew James Edward Austen-Leigh tells us in his book *Memoir of Jane Austen*, when Austen took to writing seriously at Chawton, she did not want anyone outside her family to find out that she was a writer, not even the servants. She wrote on small sheets of paper that she could easily cover with another sheet of paper or hide if anyone came in. A door that led into the room creaked when anyone opened it, but Austen didn't want the hinges fixed because the noise gave her a warning that someone was coming.

Austen hid the fact that she was a writer from the household help and from the public—all of her books

Jane Austen's sitting room at Chawton Cottage, the room where she revised *Sense and Sensibility* from a teenager's sketches into a classic novel. Undated photograph used on a 1975 postcard.

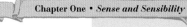

were published anonymously during her lifetime. It's unknown whether she withheld her name to avoid public judgment or whether it was just in her personality to keep to herself. But keep to herself she did.

Jane Austen makes her voice heard

With such a chilly climate in regard to women's writing, an unpublished author like Jane Austen had to navigate carefully between her culture's rejection of outspoken, critical women and her own desire to tell the story of vulnerable women that she knew all too well. So *Sense and Sensibility* is a novel with lessons to teach the reader, a proper and accepted form, and in it a young lady learns how to conduct herself. But the novel still has its rebellious elements. The author voices a quiet protest as the Dashwood women are expelled from Norland, as the greedy Mr. and Mrs. John Dashwood descend on the estate and take it over when the girls' father has barely gone cold. Austen witheringly depicts the Dashwoods' selfish natures in the first chapter of the book, portraying the gentleman and his lady as immoral: the man wavers over keeping his promise to his father, and his wife, a Lady Macbeth without the dagger, helps convince him to forget his responsibility to a dying man and his vulnerable step-mother and half-sisters.

These two vultures, along with the insipid Lady Middleton, the loud busybody Mrs. Jennings, the

SENSE

AND

SENSIBILITY:

A NOVEL.

IN THREE VOLUMES.

◆

BY A LADY.

◆

VOL. I.

London:

PRINTED FOR THE AUTHOR.

By C. Roworth, Bell-yard, Temple-bar,

AND PUBLISHED BY T. EGERTON, WHITEHALL.

1811.

Title page of the first edition of *Sense and Sensibility*, 1811, with the author credited only as "A Lady."

jovial but purposeless Sir Middleton, and the rude Mr. Palmer and stupid Mrs. Palmer, all suggest that the gentry class is full of useless and often cruelly thoughtless people. They're not all as deserving of respect as their social positions would suggest.

Young Marianne also rebels against the idea that money can matter as much as it does. We see her protest the importance of finances when she sees Willoughby at the party in London with his rich lady. Marianne's rebellion comes to an end that night, but she makes her point.

> Yes, we readers agree that Marianne must develop some self-control and learn some other lessons, but we also absorb Marianne's—and Austen's—protest against a society that places so much value on income, an income that women can't make for themselves.

"It reflects honour on the writer"

The book as a whole is an accomplishment, and though modern critics sometimes dismiss *Sense and Sensibility*, most readers would agree with a reviewer at the *Critical Review*, who said this of *Sense and Sensibility* in February 1812:

> We are no enemies to novels or to novel writers, but we regret, that in the multiplicity of them, there are so few worthy of any particular commendation. . . . *Sense and Sensibility* is one amongst the few, which can claim this fair praise. It is well written; the characters are in genteel life, naturally drawn, and judiciously

Sense and Sensibility is a novel with lessons to teach the reader, a proper and accepted form, but there are still rebellious elements.

supported. The incidents are probable, and highly pleasing, and interesting; the conclusion such as the reader must wish it should be, and the whole is just long enough to interest without fatiguing. It reflects honour on the writer, who displays much knowledge of character, and very happily blends a great deal of good sense with the lighter matter of the piece.

This was the first published review of Austen's first novel, and it must have delighted her. Even before the first printing of *Sense and Sensibility* sold out, Jane Austen knew she had arrived. She was a published author at last.

PRIDE AND PREJUDICE

"It is a truth universally acknowledged, that a single man
in possession of a good fortune, must be in want of a wife."

In January 1813, the proud author Jane Austen

wrote to her sister Cassandra, plainly thrilled to see her second novel in print: "I want to tell you that I have got my own darling Child from London;—on Wednesday I received one Copy . . ." Her excitement in her letters over *Pride and Prejudice* is even greater than over her first novel, *Sense and Sensibility*. It's clear that she loved her book.

Austen's "darling Child" took a long time to arrive: she first began the novel in October of 1796, before her twenty-first birthday, calling it at that time *First Impressions*. She finished the first draft in August, 1797. In November, her father tried to get *First Impressions* published but failed: apparently the publisher he sent it to rejected it without reading it.

The Austens move to Bath

Austen wrote *First Impressions* at Steventon in the house where she grew up: it was a lively, crowded place for the five brothers and two sisters. But in 1801 everything changed: Mr. and Mrs. Austen and their two daughters moved to Bath. Austen's brothers did not go with them, since they had established lives and homes of their own. Bath was one of England's most fashionable cities. People began to flock to the hot springs in the 1700s to

Illustration of a woman in period clothing, *Morning dress of embroidered clear lawn*, 1819, from *Rudolph Ackermann's Repository of Arts*, published in 1822.

drink the water, which was thought to have healing properties, and it was a popular place to see and be seen. But Austen did not like Bath. The tedious process of finding a new house was time-consuming, and she complains about their new acquaintances. Soon after arriving in Bath in May 1801, Jane vents

For all its playfulness and comedy and romance, this novel conveys just how vulnerable women were in Austen's world.

in a letter to Cassandra, who had not yet arrived in their new home: "Another stupid party last night." She goes on to say that she cannot find people agreeable in Bath, and adds a few biting specifics.

> "I respect Mrs. Chamberlayne for doing her hair well, but cannot feel a more tender sentiment.—Miss Langley is like any other short girl with a broad nose & wide mouth, fashionable dress, & exposed bosom."

While living in Bath, Austen apparently wrote little, ignoring *First Impressions* for years. But as soon as the Austen women moved back to Hampshire, to Chawton Cottage, in 1809, Austen began writing again. Sometime late in 1811, she revised *First Impressions* into *Pride and Prejudice*. She sold *Pride and Prejudice* to a publisher in 1812, and the book appeared in January 1813, more than fifteen years after she first began writing it. Though the book is nearly two hundred years old, readers still love it as much as ever; there's something immortal about the characters and storyline, which is by turns humorous and sobering.

Marriage and money

The plot centers on the witty, insightful, and lovable heroine Elizabeth Bennet; the cad George Wickham, who fools a whole community into thinking he's respectable; the sweet Jane Bennet and her romance with the impressionable but good-hearted Charles Bingley; and the rich, handsome, and proud Fitzwilliam Darcy, who needs to develop some self-awareness before he can correct the misconceptions Elizabeth has formed about him. Against all odds and after many missteps, Elizabeth and Darcy end up together.

One of the major obstacles to Elizabeth's happiness with Darcy is her family. As in *Sense and Sensibility*, we again find sisters caught in an unpromising situation. The

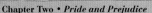

five Bennet girls have no brother and therefore no male heir, so the family will eventually lose their home. When Mr. Bennet dies, a cousin, the young clergyman Mr. Collins, will take over the estate at Longbourn. The estate earns two thousand pounds per year for the family; all of that money will go to Mr. Collins after he inherits. So the only way the Bennet women can avoid moving to a far smaller home or living with relatives is for one or more of the daughters to marry well. This will be difficult, since the family has little money to offer any of the girls as a dowry.

Marriage in Austen's time often had more to do with money than true love; a young gentry woman without money had little chance of marrying a rich gentleman, despite being members of the same class. Since marriage was so important to a woman's success, Austen's penniless female characters in *Pride and Prejudice* have little direct control over their fates. Austen writes realistically: women of her world did have little say in their own lives, and Austen wants us to notice this. *Pride and Prejudice*, for all its playfulness and comedy and romance, conveys just how vulnerable women were in Austen's world. We need only look at Elizabeth and her older sister Jane for proof of this. They are intelligent young women of wit, insight, and generosity. But such traits make little difference, for they cannot use their abilities to shape their futures. They must rely on their attractiveness and what little help their family can give them—and hope that a good man notices them.

In the Depth of Winter by Frederick Cayley Robinson, circa 1890. For women of Austen's era, marriage was practically the only way to improve their situations.

Mrs. Bennet makes another bid for Mr. Bennet's attention in an illustration by Hugh Thompson, circa 1880.

All in the family

The Bennet home is a complex place—there is love there, but not between Mr. and Mrs. Bennet. Mr. Bennet married a pretty face before noting that there wasn't much more to his wife. His character is a stroke of genius. Indolent, intelligent, and a master of satire, he loves his quick-witted second daughter Elizabeth and to a lesser extent the sweet-natured oldest girl, Jane—but he doesn't particularly love his ignorant younger daughters. He's an uneven father. He respects his Jane and Lizzy and treats them well, but his younger daughters are silly and he tells them so repeatedly. Cruel as humor often is, we laugh as he insults them. After all, they really are frivolous and self-involved. Never mind that Mr. Bennet's treatment of them leaves them all the more likely to grow up hopelessly superficial—he's *funny* as he dismisses them.

Somewhat oddly, Mr. Bennet remains very likeable, perhaps because he treats his wife as we would like to treat the Mrs. Bennets in our own lives. Mrs. Bennet is utterly self-involved, transparent, unintelligent, self-aggrandizing, and a hypochondriac. She embodies so many traits we don't like in others that it's difficult to summon any sympathy for her. Mr. Bennet sees all of this and treats her accordingly. An example: Mrs. Bennet thoughtlessly scolds one of her younger daughters for coughing, saying: "'Don't keep coughing so, Kitty, for heaven's sake! Have a little compassion on my nerves. You tear them to pieces.'" Mr. Bennet does not miss the opportunity to comment wryly on his wife's absurd demand: "'Kitty has no discretion in her coughs,' said her father, "she times them ill.'" A modern marriage counselor would quickly point out that barbs such as these put as much of a wedge between the married couple as does their basic incompatibility. But we readers, though we might be glad that we're not married to a Mr. Bennet, laugh aloud as he spews out his witty observations and retorts. In a mean little way, we as readers want him to be cruel to the myopic and shrill Mrs. Bennet. When he satirically dismisses her, we readers can vicariously dismiss the Mrs. Bennets in our own worlds.

Mrs. Bennet and her three younger daughters also rarely behave properly in social situations.

> *Today, it's not a disaster to have an embarrassing family, but in Austen's time it could reflect on every family member's reputation.*

Mrs. Bennet often humiliates the elder Bennet sisters, Jane and Elizabeth, who have somehow learned proper manners on their own. Fitzwilliam Darcy has reason to dislike Mrs. Bennet on first meeting her, and we can't blame him for thinking twice before connecting himself to this family.

Meet the Bachelors

Darcy is one of four young single men who enter the novel in its early chapters, each one seeming to offer the Bennet girls a chance at security and maybe even happiness. But when Darcy enters the story, a connection with the Bennets is simply not a possibility. At first he is only a visitor in the Bennets' village of Meryton, come to stay with his friend Bingley, who has just rented the Netherfield estate. Darcy acts arrogantly nonchalant toward Elizabeth when they first see each other at a ball; he dismisses her as only of "tolerable" appearance, within her hearing. Naturally, Elizabeth dislikes him right away. Matters between them are not promising.

But Elizabeth's older sister Jane gets along swimmingly with Darcy's friend Bingley, eligible bachelor No. 2, who has a pretty good income himself. His sisters, who are visiting him, like Jane well enough, and invite her to call on them at Netherfield. Jane falls ill while there and can't travel home, so Elizabeth walks three miles in iffy weather to help her sister. She stays at Netherfield until Jane recovers and is often in the company of the snobbish Bingley sisters and Darcy, who has a

ENVELOPE CONTENTS

- *Illustrations* by Hugh Thomson from a 19th century edition of *Pride and Prejudice*, including:

  Elizabeth overhears Mr. Darcy's dismissal at the ball.

  In the garden at Netherfield, Elizabeth leaves Mr. Bingley's sisters with Mr. Darcy and runs off alone.

  Elizabeth meets Mr. Darcy's sister Georgiana for the first time, with Mr. Darcy and Mr. Bingley.

  Mr. Bennet hands Elizabeth and Jane the letter bearing the news of Lydia's salvation.

  Elizabeth finishes her performance at Lucas Lodge.

Illustration from *Pride and Prejudice* depicting the haughty Bingley sisters turning up their noses at Elizabeth, by Hugh Thomson, circa 1880.

high opinion of his own rank and shows it. In spite of himself, the stiffly respectable Darcy begins to enjoy Elizabeth's lively, intelligent conversation. Bingley and Jane, meanwhile, grow increasingly attached to each other, although sweet, modest Jane is confined to her bedroom.

Darcy and the Bingley sisters notice Bingley's interest in Jane, and they also notice the bad behavior of Mrs. Bennet and her two youngest daughters (and the girls' eagerness to flirt with the military officers stationed in town). So Darcy and Bingley's sisters work to sabotage the developing relationship between Bingley and Jane. But Darcy's feelings toward Elizabeth are also growing—at a ball that Bingley hosts at Netherfield, they dance together, and he can't help but admire her as she engages him in some of the repartee that this couple is famous for.

"It *is your* turn to say something now, Mr. Darcy.—I talked about the dance, and *you* ought to make some kind of remark on the size of the room, or the number of the couples."

He smiled, and assured her that whatever she wished him to say should be said.

"Very well.—That reply will do for the present.—Perhaps by and bye I may observe that private balls are much pleasanter than public ones.—But *now* we may be silent."

"Do you talk by rule then, while you are dancing?"

"Sometimes. One must speak a little, you know. It would look odd to be entirely silent for half an hour together, and yet for the advantage of *some*, conversation ought to be so arranged as that they may have the trouble of saying as little as possible."

In spite of himself, the stiffly respectable Darcy begins to enjoy Elizabeth's lively, intelligent conversation.

"Are you consulting your own feelings in the present case, or do you imagine that you are gratifying mine?"

"Both," replied Elizabeth archly; "for I have always seen a great similarity in the turn of our minds.— We are each of an unsocial, taciturn disposition, unwilling to speak, unless we expect to say something that will amaze the whole room, and be handed down to posterity with all the éclat of a proverb."

When Elizabeth and Darcy engage in conversations like these, the rest of the dancers—and the rest of the world—

just disappear; we see only the couple, one drawn against his will and the other repelled but intrigued, trying to come to an understanding of one another.

Many women have danced a relational tango with a Mr. Wickham—if they're lucky, they'll wake up before he does any serious harm.

Wickham's story

One of the tense topics between Elizabeth and Darcy is Mr. George Wickham, the third young man who comes into the neighborhood; he is one of the officers stationed in Meryton. He initially charms everyone in the area with his good looks and easygoing personality. But he later reveals himself as irresponsible and uncommitted, a classic rake who piles up debts. Wickham is a Peter Pan with a gambling problem. Many women have danced a relational tango with a Mr. Wickham—if they're

lucky, they'll wake up before he does any serious harm. While he still has everybody's good opinion, Wickham tells Elizabeth a half-true tale about Mr. Darcy, claiming that Darcy has seriously wronged him by preventing him from becoming a clergyman and earning a respectable income. On hearing Wickham's tale, Elizabeth, who already dislikes Darcy and favors Wickham, decides that she dislikes him fiercely.

The first proposal

Mr. Collins is the fourth man to enter the neighborhood, and he is even more fun to despise than Mrs. Bennet: he's pompous and sanctimonious, without an ounce of self-awareness in his being. His alternating fawning and vain ranting, his false morality and shallow feelings—they all repulse us. He's also single and looking for a wife.

Mr. Collins has heard of his five female cousins at Longbourn, and he's happy enough to marry one of them; given he'll one day take their home, the idea appeals to his sense of himself as a generous, charitable, and desirable man. He focuses on Elizabeth and proposes. Elizabeth, an intelligent, perceptive woman, immediately turns him down—it would be too ridiculous to marry such a fool. We're relieved when Elizabeth rejects him, despite her thoughtless mother's pressure to accept him, and

Mr. Collins proposes to Elizabeth in an illustration by Hugh Thomson, circa 1880.

Chapter Two • *Pride and Prejudice*

even happier when Mr. Bennet wittily aligns with Elizabeth as she denies Mr. Collins: "'An unhappy alternative is before you, Elizabeth. From this day

Elizabeth insists on loving the man she marries—and by doing this, she rebels against her culture's unwritten rules for women.

you must be a stranger to one of your parents.— Your mother will never see you again if you do *not* marry Mr. Collins, and I will never see you again if you *do*.'"

"As delightful a creature as ever appeared in print"

The truth is, from a pragmatic perspective, Elizabeth is wrong to refuse this marriage proposal. Mr. Collins is, after all, a man of money and reputation. Given her culture and her family's financial state, Elizabeth should have taken the

comfortable home that Mr. Collins offers her. From the gentry's social perspective, marrying a ridiculous man is better than becoming a spinster, and for a single woman to know that she is a financial burden on her family is ignominious and emotionally draining. But Elizabeth won't accept Mr. Collins's proposal, in spite of the fact that Mr. Collins will inherit her family home and her father's two thousand pounds per year. She insists on loving the man she marries— and by doing this, she rebels against her culture's unwritten rules for women.

This rebellion is partly why readers admire Elizabeth Bennet: she sticks to her principles and does so with wit and grace. Austen was undeniably happy with her nonconformist heroine, as she demonstrates in a letter to Cassandra:

> "... I must confess that I think her as delightful a creature as ever appeared in print, & how I shall be able to tolerate those who do not like her at least, I do not know."

Austen contrasts her beloved Elizabeth with Charlotte Lucas, Elizabeth's best friend, who does the sensible thing when it comes to marriage. Immediately after Elizabeth rejects him, Mr. Collins transfers his amorous attention to Charlotte—and he finds success.

We readers like Charlotte. What you see is what you get in her. Today she would be a trustworthy locker mate in high school, but she'd also be the friend who doesn't get asked out much. She's too honest, and—sigh—probably too intelligent as well. In our world she would work hard in school and at her job and do fine on her own, even if she never married. But in her own time, Charlotte has no opportunity to shape her own destiny. So she pragmatically weighs her options as she nears age thirty, what Austen calls in *Persuasion* the "years of danger" for an unmarried woman. And then she agrees to marry her best friend's cousin. Her acceptance will remove a financial burden from her family and give her some independence. We readers understand this. But still…Mr. Collins?

Austen's own proposal

Austen knew all too well how strong the drive to escape dependence on one's family could be. She herself nearly did what Charlotte did—marry a man she didn't love because of the position and wealth he could give her. In December 1802, Harris Bigg-Wither, the brother of some close friends of hers, proposed to Jane Austen. He was five years younger than she, and he spoke with a stammer. But as Claire Tomalin tells us, Austen had many reasons to accept Bigg-Wither's proposal: she would become mistress of a fine large house, she would live in her home county

Mr. Collins assures Elizabeth of his affection "in the most animated language." Illustration by Hugh Thompson, circa 1880.

of Hampshire, and she would be able to provide for her parents and sister. So the night he proposed, Austen said yes. But the next day, she ended the engagement. She couldn't do the "right" thing by her family and for her future without having her heart involved.

Elizabeth the rebel

Given Austen's own personality, it's no surprise that Elizabeth Bennet is not purely sweet and kind like her sister Jane, nor practical like Charlotte Lucas—so of course she has to refuse Mr. Collins. Elizabeth is, in fact, one of the first rebel heroines in English literature, and one of the first to recognize her own faults and grow as a person. She is neither the angelic heroine nor the evil scheming or fallen woman found in earlier novels. Austen's heroines do not follow the rules of society without question, and Elizabeth Bennet asks more questions than any other Austen character. Throughout the novel she rejects the unreasonable expectations of her world; we see this soon after she and Mr. Darcy meet. She is unwilling to be impressed by Darcy's power and privilege. She refuses to dance with him when he first asks her to do so, in part out of retaliation for his dismissive treatment of her at the ball where they met.

She also refuses to agree with him sycophantically, as Miss Bingley does. We first see this in a discussion of accomplished women while Elizabeth is staying

1898 illustration by H. M. Brock from *Pride and Prejudice,* showing Elizabeth playing for Colonel Fitzwilliam and Mr. Darcy.

at Netherfield. Darcy expresses high expectations of women in a long list of accomplishments and graces, to which Miss Bingley adds even more requirements. Darcy says he knows of only half a dozen women who meet his criteria. Elizabeth responds tartly: "'I am no longer surprised at your knowing *only* six accomplished women. I rather wonder now at your knowing *any*.'" Later she and Darcy spar again. Miss Bingley plays a "lively Scotch air" on the piano, which prompts Darcy to ask Elizabeth whether she does not feel the impulse to dance a reel. Darcy's question might be insulting; common folk typically danced reels. Elizabeth shoots back:

> "'You wanted me, I know, to say "Yes," that you might have the pleasure of despising my taste; but I always delight in overthrowing those kinds of schemes, and cheating a person of their premeditated contempt. I have therefore made up my mind to tell you, that I do not want to dance a reel at all—and now despise me if you dare.'"

Needless to say, Mr. Darcy does not dare.

The suitability of exercise for young ladies

Elizabeth flaunts her culture's expectations of women in other ways. She has a not-quite-proper love of activity and nature. Proper young women took their "exercise" by strolling through a garden, preferably on a man's arm. But at least once Elizabeth refuses to walk with a man; while walking with the Bingley sisters and Darcy one day at Netherfield, she chooses to go her own way: "She then ran gaily off,

Austen's heroines do not follow the rules of society without question, and Elizabeth Bennet is Austen's most rebellious heroine.

rejoicing as she rambled about. . . ." She also refuses to take the carriage to visit Jane when she is sick at Netherfield—she would rather walk the three miles. For an unmarried gentry woman to walk six miles round-trip alone wasn't considered quite appropriate in 1813. But this is Elizabeth's plan and she will act on it, though she suspects she will be criticized for her actions. She's right: the Bingley sisters do hold her in contempt for walking to Netherfield rather than taking a carriage. Mrs. Hurst says that upon arriving, Elizabeth "'really looked almost wild.'" Miss Bingley agrees and goes on to say, "'To walk three miles, or four miles, or five miles, or whatever it is, above her

The incomparable Colin Firth as Mr. Darcy and Jennifer Ehle as Elizabeth Bennet in the BBC adaptation of *Pride and Prejudice*, 1995.

ancles in dirt, and alone, quite alone! what could she mean by it? It seems to me to shew an abominable sort of conceited independence, a most country town indifference to decorum.'" Darcy, however, can't help but admire Elizabeth. Rather than condemn her for her hike to Netherfield, he notes that her eyes "'were brightened by the exercise.'"

A subtle update on film

The 1995 *Pride and Prejudice* miniseries picks up on these hints of physical attraction in the novel and expands on them in a way that draws modern audiences into the love story while staying true to Austen's time period. The miniseries team—director Simon Langton, screenwriter Andrew Davies, and actors Colin Firth and Jennifer Ehle—have probably done more to make Jane Austen popular than anyone since Austen herself. Their version of the story is a sexually charged *Pride and Prejudice*, but not unbelievably so. People of the early nineteenth century did have bodies and sexual natures, after all. Langton's version of the novel gently informs us of this; he unleashes the bodies of the nineteenth-century heroine and hero. But this happens in private, when no one else is supposed to see, which keeps it believable.

With its focus on the body, this film version of *Pride and Prejudice* reflects our own time, but Langton also respects the fact that bodies weren't at liberty in 1813. So we see Elizabeth running and skipping outside, but only when she knows no one can see her. When inside, the outdoors pulls the characters to the windows to look out. We see Darcy bathing in one scene. While drying himself, he stands looking out of the window and sees Elizabeth below playing freely and vigorously with his dog

Some readers of Austen's era rejected the novel because of Elizabeth's rebellious attitude.

when she thinks no one is looking. Langton conveys that moments like these, when Darcy watches Elizabeth move so unrestrainedly while thinking herself alone, help win Darcy's heart (and other body parts). In a world where people had to ignore their bodies but so clearly still had them, Darcy would notice a woman who was comfortable in her own skin.

This version of *Pride and Prejudice* is presented to a millennial world where we know that the facts of our bodies don't go away, whatever the cultural attitudes toward them. So Darcy fences furiously, trying to forget Elizabeth, and then strips off his coat and vest and dives into a pond, minutes before meeting her again. His body has desires that he can't satisfy; the film version suggests that Elizabeth has awakened something powerful in him.

Following along as Darcy and Elizabeth stumble toward union is one of the novel's greatest pleasures——in part because Austen guides the action so deftly.

Reactions to a "pert" heroine

Elizabeth's freedom in action as well as thought intrigues Darcy and also provides one of the main reasons modern readers and viewers find Elizabeth easy to relate to. But some readers of Austen's era rejected the novel because of Elizabeth's rebellious attitude. Consider what one reader had to say of Elizabeth Bennet. In 1814, Miss Mary Russell Mitford, a published writer herself, sent a letter to a

friend with her thoughts on *Pride and Prejudice*'s author and heroine:

> The want of elegance is almost the only want in Miss Austen. . . . it is impossible not to feel in every line of *Pride and Prejudice*, in every word of 'Elizabeth,' the entire want of taste which could produce so pert, so worldly a heroine as the beloved of such a man as Darcy. Wickham is equally bad. Oh! they were just fit for each other, and I cannot forgive that delightful Darcy for parting them. Darcy should have married Jane.

That Jane Bennet would be more popular with some readers in 1814, and that Elizabeth would be considered "pert," shows us the strict expectations of women during Austen's lifetime. But note that Darcy's appeal seems to be universal—as devoted Austen readers might expect.

But the published reviews of *Pride and Prejudice* spoke highly of the novel. Two months after the book appeared, a writer for the *Critical Review* wrote, "[There is not] one character which appears flat, or obtrudes itself upon the notice of the reader with troublesome impertinence. There is not one person in the drama with whom we could readily dispense;—they have all their proper places; and fill their several stations, with great credit to themselves, and much satisfaction to the reader." The *British Critic* published another glowing review in 1813 that Austen must have been pleased to read, saying that *Pride and Prejudice* was "very far superior to almost all the publication of the kind which have lately come before us. . . . the story is well told, the characters remarkably well drawn and supported, and written with great spirit as well as vigour."

Chance meetings

Following along as Darcy and Elizabeth stumble toward union is one of the novel's greatest pleasures—in part because Austen guides the action so deftly. A series of coincidences throw Elizabeth and Darcy together again and again, but their chance meetings don't feel artificial: Austen writes so well that her plot contrivances to pull the two protagonists together become nearly invisible. The first such contrivances occur when Bingley rents Netherfield, and Darcy comes to visit: Elizabeth unexpectedly spends several days with them, tending her sick sister Jane, and intrigues Darcy. But Darcy resists Elizabeth and tries to block Jane and Bingley's budding romance by colluding with Bingley's sisters to whisk him off to London; it appears that Bingley is not interested in Jane after all, while Darcy tries to govern his own attraction to Elizabeth.

Jane goes to London to visit family and get over her disappointment, and Elizabeth goes to visit Charlotte for a few weeks at her new home with Mr. Collins. Mr. Collins lives at the parsonage at Rosings Park; his patroness, and the most important person in the area, is Lady Catherine de Bourgh. Austen expects us to loathe her, and we do, with gusto. As with Mrs. Bennet, we can see no reason to sympathize with Lady Catherine. She is rich and pompous and meddling and insulting, the vilest character in the book. Karl Marx must have met a few Lady Catherines in the 1840s, which can only have inspired him to write *The Communist Manifesto*. If ever a character could prompt a call for the collapsing of the class system, it's Lady Catherine de Bourgh.

Another proposal

As it turns out, the despicable Lady Catherine is Darcy's aunt, and he happens to visit her while Elizabeth is at the parsonage (coincidence No. 2). They see each other often, as Lady Catherine can't help but like Elizabeth, and her own little world—with a sickly daughter her only company—doesn't offer many diversions. So she invites the unctuous Mr. Collins and his wife and friend often for dinner. After several weeks in close company, Darcy stops trying to deny his attraction to Elizabeth. He asks her to marry him, saying that he's tried to resist, but can't hold out any longer; he wants her to marry him in spite of her family. But Elizabeth does not love him, and she's angry that he has treated Mr. Wickham so poorly and worked to end the relationship between Jane and Bingley. She rejects him.

BINGLEY'S SISTERS Miss Bingley and Mrs. Hurst seem to embody the word "catty" as they try to "protect" their brother from Jane and lure Mr. Darcy away from Elizabeth. But the haughty Bingley sisters have some reason to be selfish: a culture that offered gentry women so few choices was bound to create some monstrous women. The gentry women of Britain couldn't improve their situations through hard work. Working at all was considered degrading, so marriage was the only option. The gentry woman's tools were her wits, her beauty, her talents (dancing, drawing, languages, and such), her connections, and her father's income. If any of these were missing—say a woman wasn't beautiful or had no dowry—she was in danger of embracing that nasty word "spinster."

The competition for a rich man was stiff in Britain; as scholar David Shapard tells us, with ten thousand pounds a year, Mr. Darcy is one of the one or two hundred wealthiest men in England. It's no wonder, then, that Miss Bingley tries so earnestly to derail Mr. Darcy's growing interest in Elizabeth. She needs him to prefer her to all other women—and save her from the social black hole and poverty that is spinsterhood. So we can feel some sympathy for Miss Bingley. Not much, though.

Mr. Denny asks permission to introduce his friend, Mr. Wickham. Illustration by H. M. Brock, 1898.

This is a real risk, for he is one of the richest men in England, and she has almost no money of her own. And she doesn't say no politely. She unleashes the anger she's felt for months at Darcy's haughty arrogance, telling him that he is no gentleman, and more: "'You could not have made me the offer of your hand in any possible way that would have tempted me to accept it.'" She adds "'. . . I had not known you a month before I felt that you were the last man in the world whom I could ever be prevailed on to marry.'" Saying all this to a man who is so much wealthier, who could ridicule and abuse her socially and in so doing reduce her prospects all the more, takes some courage.

So the proposal goes all wrong, and they are kept apart, because both of them continue to allow their faulty thinking to guide them. Elizabeth is still swayed by her first impressions of him and holds tightly to her hasty conclusions (prejudice), and he is still struggling with the gap between their positions and fortunes (pride). But the story's not over yet.

The road to reunion

Wounded over Elizabeth's rejection of him, Darcy writes her a long letter explaining himself: in regard to Mr. Wickham, the man actually tried to seduce and elope with Darcy's rich teenage sister. Darcy severed his family's relationship with Wickham, and that was the real reason Wickham was denied the position he was promised as clergyman. In regard to Bingley, Darcy doubted that Jane liked him, and on top of that, the Bennet family, he feels compelled to point out, is pretty socially disastrous. The letter doesn't entirely change Elizabeth's mind about Darcy, but she starts to question her intense dislike of him. They go their separate ways—but another of Jane Austen's skillful coincidences draws them together again.

Elizabeth is looking forward to a long trip up north with her aunt and uncle the Gardiners. But as

Elizabeth is still swayed by her first impressions of him (prejudice), and he is still struggling with the gap between their positions and fortunes (pride).

luck would have it, they need to cut their trip short and settle for a tour of Derbyshire, where Darcy's estate, Pemberley, is located. Mrs. Gardiner once lived in Lambton, the town nearest Pemberley, and she longs to see the grand estate, for it has "some of the finest woods in the country." Elizabeth only agrees to explore it because Darcy is out of town, but he arrives unexpectedly and meets her there.

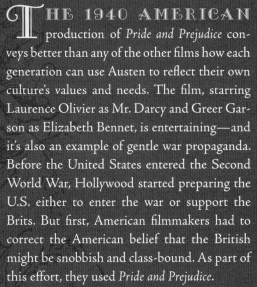

Darcy and Elizabeth During Wartime

THE 1940 AMERICAN production of *Pride and Prejudice* conveys better than any of the other films how each generation can use Austen to reflect their own culture's values and needs. The film, starring Laurence Olivier as Mr. Darcy and Greer Garson as Elizabeth Bennet, is entertaining—and it's also an example of gentle war propaganda. Before the United States entered the Second World War, Hollywood started preparing the U.S. either to enter the war or support the Brits. But first, American filmmakers had to correct the American belief that the British might be snobbish and class-bound. As part of this effort, they used *Pride and Prejudice*.

We see what a class-bound person looks like as the movie begins. Darcy rejects Elizabeth at the ball as he does in the book, dismissing her as "tolerable." But his reasons for rejecting her have changed somewhat. Rather than announce, "I am in no humour at present to give consequence to young ladies who are slighted by other men," which is Austen's line, the Darcy of the 1940 film says, "I'm in no humor tonight to give consequence to the middle classes at play." Ah—Darcy is a worse snob than we thought—he dismisses the middle classes. But Elizabeth can fix this. Later in the film, at a garden party, Elizabeth bests him at archery, shooting several bull's-eyes in a row after he has failed to shoot accurately. The "middle classes at play" have bested the upper-class guy. But there's hope for Darcy, for he takes this lesson well. "Next time I talk to a young lady about archery," he says ruefully, "I won't be so patronizing."

Most notably, Lady Catherine de Bourgh gets some democratic modernizing in the film. Near the film's end, she comes as usual to Longbourn to deliver her speech demanding that Elizabeth surrender her relationship with Darcy. But she adds a wrinkle that Austen never thought of: she claims that she is actually the trustee of Pemberley, that she can strip Darcy of all his money, and that she'll do it if he marries Elizabeth. This threat does nothing to change Elizabeth's mind. If Darcy asks her to marry him, she will do so, even if the two of them become paupers afterward. Lady Catherine then leaves the house, and—here's an even bigger not-in-the-book moment—Darcy is waiting for her in the carriage. He brought Lady Catherine to Longbourn, it turns out, to test Elizabeth. As she climbs into the carriage, Darcy ascertains

Pemberley impresses Elizabeth, and she can't help but contemplate the fact that she could have been the mistress of the fine property.

> *Devoted Austen readers don't like to dwell on this, but there is plenty of evidence that Elizabeth comes to see Darcy in a more positive light when she stands in his home and absorbs the immensity of his money and property and power.*

She finally realizes whom she has rejected. As any self-aware person should, Elizabeth herself recognizes the power Darcy's position has had on her. When Jane later asks her, after hearing of her engagement to Darcy, how long she has loved him, Elizabeth answers bluntly: "It has been coming on so gradually, that I hardly know when it began. But I believe I must date it from my first seeing his beautiful grounds at Pemberley." Though she says this half-jokingly, Elizabeth does feel the possibilities of being married to one of the richest men in the land.

It's not only money, though, that changes her mind. She finds herself liking Darcy better as they spend time together at Pemberley—he has changed his outward behavior and is respectful toward her and her aunt and uncle. She meets Georgiana,

Darcy's sister, and the two young women like each other. Promise is in the air.

A scandal, and a rescue

Then disaster strikes: Elizabeth receives a letter from Jane saying that Wickham has run off with the youngest and most ignorant Bennet sister, Lydia. He is clearly not after her money, and he has not married her. They hole up in London where, we assume, Wickham enjoys himself with a sixteen-year-old girl. Lydia's action will bring social censure to the entire family. Darcy happens upon Elizabeth as she reads Jane's letter—she weeps as she tells him the evil news. Elizabeth despairs that there will be no chance for Jane to wed Bingley now and that Darcy will soon forget her.

But quietly, Darcy fixes everything. He goes to London, finds Wickham, and essentially bribes him into marrying Lydia, smoothing over that problem. Then he brings Bingley back to the Meryton area where Bingley and Jane quickly reunite and become engaged.

Elizabeth soon receives a surprise visit from Darcy's aunt Lady Catherine; she demands to know whether Elizabeth is engaged to Darcy. Elizabeth says she is not. Lady Catherine commands Elizabeth to promise that she will not marry Darcy, as he is expected to marry her daughter, his first cousin. Lady Catherine has no claim on Elizabeth other than the fact that she is wealthier and used to being obeyed—but even though

that their ruse has worked: Lady Catherine tells him that she threatened Elizabeth and she stood firm: she intends to marry Darcy even if he's a poor man, revealing that she does indeed love him. Darcy gives her a big hug.

So Lady Catherine was on the side of the middle classes all along! The message to American viewers is clear: the British do care about democratic ideals. The U.S. isn't going to war to help save an aristocracy—they're going to war to help the adorable Lizzie Bennet and her soon-to-be aunt-in-law, the chummy Cathy Bourgh.

The film is worth seeing: the comic elements and central lessons are still there, and the revealing effort to make our allies look more like ourselves has historical relevance in and of itself.

Greer Garson as Elizabeth Bennet and Lawrence Olivier as Mr. Darcy in the 1940 adaptation of *Pride and Prejudice*.

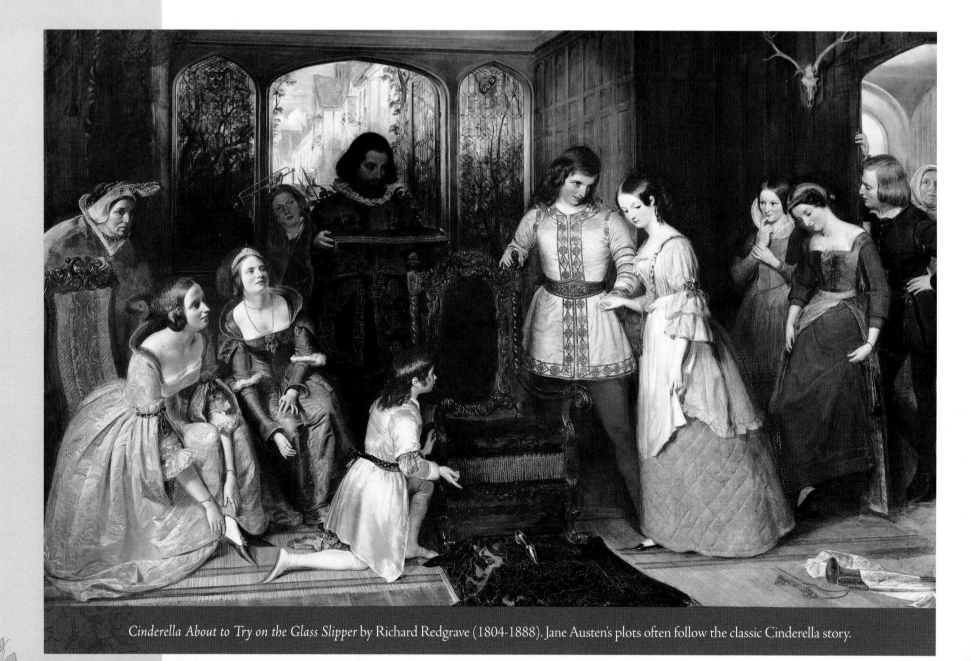

Cinderella About to Try on the Glass Slipper by Richard Redgrave (1804-1888). Jane Austen's plots often follow the classic Cinderella story.

Elizabeth still doubts that Darcy will propose, she will not give in to Lady Catherine. She refuses to say she will not marry Darcy.

On hearing this, Darcy takes his chance to try again, the right way this time, and at long last he and Elizabeth become engaged.

The Cinderella story

As attentive readers are prone to notice, in *Pride and Prejudice* and other of her novels, Austen often presents a classic Cinderella story: a deserving and intelligent woman struggles and appears to be doomed to an awful fate because she is poor. No matter how kind and generous and intelligent and capable the character is, for her to succeed in life, as her culture defines success, she needs a Prince Charming: a rich, kind man who will see beyond the woman's limited financial circumstances or family reputation and recognize her beauty and character. If a Prince Charming doesn't arrive, the fine woman must rely on the kindness of family and friends. Not finding that, she must rely on the kindness of strangers—and hope that she can find a good position as a governess. All of Austen's Cinderella characters sit in a precarious position, hoping for a proposal to save them from a life of "degradation" as an employee rather than a wife.

This type of story is not as popular today as it once was. This is in part because it isn't so necessary. The downtrodden woman has less reason to need a fairy tale in which everything turns out all right after a man rides to the rescue. Women today have far more authority over their own fates: they too can pull themselves up by their bootstraps—at least in the developed world. But even though things have improved, characters like Elizabeth and Jane are still important: they offer a window into women's lives before hard-won rights gave them more options.

All of Austen's Cinderella characters sit in a precarious position, hoping for a proposal to save them from a life of "degradation" as an employee rather than a wife.

"A woman may take liberties with her husband"

Elizabeth and Darcy's union is a Cinderella story to some extent, but it's more than that—they share a two-way relationship. Elizabeth proves her mettle throughout the novel, as she refuses to bow down to anyone, even to her powerful husband once they are married.

Sir William Lucas urges Darcy to dance with Elizabeth at a party at Lucas Lodge. He is willing, but she is not. Illustration by H. M. Brock, 1898.

> *"Georgiana had the highest opinion in the world of Elizabeth; though at first she often listened with an astonishment bordering on alarm, at her lively, sportive, manner of talking to her brother. . . . By Elizabeth's instructions she began to comprehend that a woman may take liberties with her husband, which a brother will not always allow in a sister more than ten years younger than himself."*

The law, as we know, is entirely on the man's side in a nineteenth-century marriage, but Elizabeth has established as best possible for her era an equal relationship, one that readers of the twenty-first century can still relate to. There's a lesson in this, too.

The coupling of Darcy and Elizabeth satisfies the reader in part because the reader knows that each has saved the other. Darcy has saved Elizabeth from marrying a Mr. Collins or a Mr. Wickham or from being a financial burden to her family. He's also saved her from her own assumptions by helping her to face herself. After his first proposal, she owns that she was wrong to believe Wickham without considering that there is always another side to a story. She recognizes that Wickham's charm and good looks made her forget her common sense,

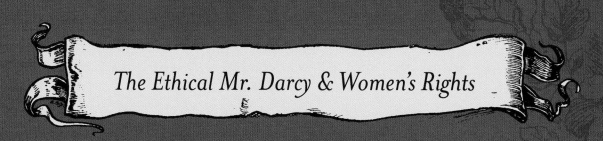

The Ethical Mr. Darcy & Women's Rights

JANE AUSTEN CHOSE her beloved Lizzy Bennet's husband carefully. Darcy is a morally sound man who does the right thing: he protects his sister from the dissolute Wickham, then later salvages the situation between Wickham and Lydia. One of the reasons Austen makes Darcy so ethical, so stiffly upright, is this: a man with such morals would be far less likely to treat his wife unfairly.

British law in regard to women was highly restrictive during Austen's lifetime. As defined by the English jurist William Blackstone in the eighteenth century, once married, a woman became a *feme covert* (a "covered woman"), which meant that her legal existence disappeared. Legally, she became an appendage of her husband—she was under his "cover." Because she had no legal existence of her own, a married woman's personal property became her husband's. A kind and judicious husband might respect his wife's right to her own money, but the law did not require him to do so. There

was one exception: a woman continued to own any land she brought to the marriage, but, as Daniel Pool tells us, if the land made any income, the husband got the money. Husbands also controlled any wages their wives earned, and even had a right to imprison their wives in their own homes. A husband controlled the children as well—even if he was an alcoholic or wife beater or child abuser—and women could never easily divorce, because it was expensive and social and legal opinion was against them. As Pool puts it, "of the ninety parliamentary divorces granted before 1857, women obtained only four."

In a world where men could legally treat their wives viciously, anyone who cares about Elizabeth Bennet wants to see her marry a man who has rigidly fair values. And Darcy lives up to this: he's a knight in shining armor, a Prince Charming. At least one Austenite has named a beloved male cat after Fitzwilliam Darcy. (That would be me.)

as did her hurt feelings when she was rejected by Mr. Darcy the first time he saw her. She also faces the fact that her family does act inappropriately at times, and that if she notices it, should she be surprised and offended that others do as well?

Elizabeth saves Darcy from his own privileges. When we first meet Mr. Darcy, he is a snob, a man concerned about appearances and wealth. When

> *Millions of readers have fallen in love with Darcy because he falls in love with Elizabeth for all the right reasons.*

he dismisses Elizabeth as being "tolerable; but not handsome enough to tempt *me*," he must know that she is within earshot, or he *should* know it. But he is the richest person in the room, secure in the knowledge that no one can hurt him socially or economically—this is the case just about wherever he goes. Such power has made him hypocritical and elitist.

Darcy conveys to us how much money matters in his culture. If the Bennets had more money attached to them than the relatively small amount of two thousand pounds a year, and if their property were not entailed to Mr. Collins, Darcy might have overlooked the

unseemly behavior of Mrs. Bennet and her younger daughters, just as he overlooks the rude behavior of his aunt Lady Catherine and Bingley's sisters. Austen's message here is that finances determine value in this culture and to some degree perception of a person's character. Therefore, to Darcy, Mrs. Bennet is offensive and her younger daughters intolerable. But rich Lady Catherine, who displays an uglier character than Mrs. Bennet and acts just as reprehensibly, is acceptable enough to receive a visit from him.

But because of Elizabeth, Darcy faces himself. In the end, he has the sense to love a worthwhile woman. Millions of readers have fallen in love with Darcy because he falls in love with Elizabeth for all the right reasons. He loves her for her personality, not her good looks (though he eventually decides that she is "one of the handsomest women of my acquaintance"). He loves her because she is lively and intelligent and unafraid of him. And when Elizabeth is most defeated by life—when her unmarried sister Lydia runs off to London with a man—Darcy quietly and unasked corrects the situation.

These two big personalities change and adapt in order to accommodate each other. They are not perfect characters, but they become self-aware enough to own their mistakes and change as necessary. When fallible but likeable characters make mistakes and then face those mistakes, we like them all the more. They demonstrate to us that we can address our own problems as bravely as they do. And, when it's attached to a good love story, who minds learning a lesson?

Fanny and Jane Hamond by Sir Thomas Lawrence (1769-1830).

Chapter Three

MANSFIELD PARK

"There certainly are not so many men of large fortune in
the world, as there are pretty women to deserve them."

Unlike her previous two published novels,

Sense and Sensibility and *Pride and Prejudice*, which she started when she was still in her teens, Austen wrote *Mansfield Park* entirely as an adult. She wrote over a period of two and a half years from 1811 to 1813, and the novel was published the year after *Pride and Prejudice*, in May 1814. She was thirty-five years old when she started the novel, and we see in it a more mature writer's determination to develop her art.

Mansfield Park is an ambitious project: Austen tries several new approaches simultaneously. As is easy to do with an Austen novel, a reader can slide past these innovations without seeing them while absorbing the characters or the clever language. But when we look closer, the significance of Austen's experiments becomes clear.

Jane Austen's experiments

Jane Austen's first new approach in *Mansfield Park* is immediately obvious: she presents a more intense realism than she had previously portrayed for her readers. Of all Austen's central characters, we see only Fanny Price as a girl, and she is a girl from a relatively poor background. We get a glimpse of her struggling family in Portsmouth at the beginning of the novel, and

At Her Desk, a representation of a female writer by Henry Thomas Schafer, late 1800s.

we see the impoverished child handed over to her aunt's cold family, the Bertrams. We watch as Mrs. Norris, Fanny's nasty aunt and the most mean-spirited of all Austen's characters, undermines little Fanny's confidence at every turn. We see her harsh uncle Sir Thomas Bertram try to manipulate his niece into compliance. We see Sir Thomas's

Jane Austen's innovations hint at what Charles Dickens and George Eliot would do later on in the century.

eldest son presented as a drunken gambler, and we see his daughter leave her husband because of her sexual attraction to another man—and later we see her husband divorce her. All of these elements explore a grimmer side of life in a way that was rarely seen in the fiction of Austen's time. Austen also engages in a mild ideological critique: we see overt praise of men who succeed because of merit rather than inheritance (we will see this again in *Persuasion*). These are new elements both for Jane

Austen and for English literature in general; Jane Austen's innovations hint at what Charles Dickens and George Eliot would do later on in the century.

"The simple regimen of separate bedrooms"

Jane Austen also shows the consequences of having many children, which was perhaps an indelicate subject for her readers but a very real problem in 1814. By the time she wrote *Mansfield Park*, Austen knew all about large families. Her own family of eight children did not have much money, and her brother Edward fathered eleven children. Edward's sister-in-law Sophia and her husband William Deedes had twenty children. The birth of their eighteenth child, Marianne, in 1817 prompted Austen to observe the following in a letter to her niece Fanny Knight, "Good Mrs. Deedes!—I hope she will get the better of this Marianne, & then I wd recommend to her & Mr. D. the simple regimen of separate bedrooms." Austen would likely have recommended that Fanny Price's parents try separate bedrooms too, as abstinence was the only acceptable form of birth control available during Austen's lifetime. But Mr. and Mrs. Price could not sleep in separate bedrooms, of course; their crowded house in Portsmouth would not allow for any such effort at family planning. So the babies kept coming.

In defense of the clergy

Another innovation in *Mansfield Park* concerns Austen's effort to present the clergy in a more positive light than she has in previous novels. Each of Austen's novels has a clergyman or future clergyman present, but until she published *Mansfield Park*, she had never presented a member of the clergy as a solid spiritual guide. The most obvious parson she must make up for is *Pride and Prejudice*'s Mr. Collins, the most laughable and odious character in Austen's novels. In *Sense and Sensibility*, Edward Ferrars will become a clergyman soon, but he shows no real piety, though he certainly shows integrity (any man who would grit his teeth and stay engaged to Lucy Steele has a high sense of ethics indeed). With Edward, Austen portrays the office of the clergy as an opportunity to achieve an income and social position rather than as a spiritual calling; his lack of religious mission is noticeable. *Northanger Abbey* had not been published yet (though it was finished), but that novel's clergyman, Henry Tilney, also does not come across as particularly pious.

In all of Austen, we never see a parson at work, writing or giving a sermon or advising a member of his congregation. We don't see scenes unfolding in churches, though churches are alluded to, and we don't see people appealing to God. It seems telling that in *Mansfield Park*, Austen's fourth complete major novel, she finally creates a man who appears suited for the real work of the clergy, after portraying one mighty silly parson and two indifferent ones. It's also telling that after writing *Mansfield Park*, Austen returns to portraying the clergy as feckless and vain (Mr. Elton in *Emma*) or indifferent (in *Persuasion*, parson-to-be Charles Hayter doesn't appear pious, nor is there any sign that Captain Wentworth's unseen clergyman brother is a deeply devoted man).

But *Mansfield Park*'s Edmund Bertram is a person of strong moral fiber from the moment we first see him. He does right by all, is honest and upstanding, and tries to help others. Unlike Austen's other rectors and parish priests, Edmund has personal traits that make him particularly appropriate for the clergy.

The clergymen in Austen's life

By choosing to write more positively of the clergy in this way, Jane Austen likely was expressing a loyalty to the clergymen in her own family. Her father was a rector, and two of her brothers became clergymen. Her brother James, the eldest Austen child, went to Oxford and later became a curate; later still, when his father retired to Bath, James took over his father's two livings and moved into the Austens' Steventon home with his family. Austen's favorite brother Henry also went to Oxford and also planned to become a clergyman, but he veered off into the military and then banking before becoming a curate and eventually

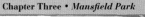

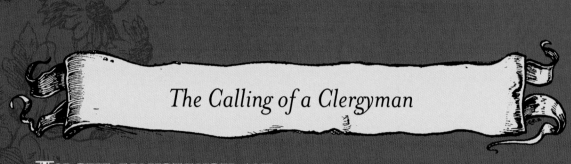

The Calling of a Clergyman

IN THE EIGHTEENTH AND nineteenth centuries, a position as a clergyman in Britain was as much about social position as it was about religious devotion and a desire to help others. The Church of England was a powerful social and financial entity in the country that had the right to tithe parishioners. Tithing meant that all those living within a parish were expected to give ten percent of their income to the Church, usually in the form of farm produce in Austen's lifetime. This income supported the rector or vicar or curate in the area who would conduct Sunday services, perform weddings and christenings, attend to the poor, and more.

What's the difference between a rector and a vicar and a curate? This is rather complicated. The rector has the best position—he is paid the most and has full control of the income of a living; that is, he gets the full tithes of a given area. The vicar or curate serves in the place of the rector because rectors don't have to live in the area where they serve. These absent rectors would hire a local clergyman—a vicar or curate—to perform religious duties in a given

parish. Because a vicar is hired by a rector, he earns a portion of the rector's pay. The curate does the most work for the least pay—he does much of the work of a rector, but for an even smaller portion of the rector's pay. Thus a curate hopes to one day become a rector himself, with help from his connections to influential friends and family members.

Typically second sons or other younger sons became clergymen; it was a way for them to make a respectable living, given that only firstborn sons could inherit the family estate. (Other respectable ways of making a living for non-firstborn sons included going into law or joining the military.) To become a clergyman, one usually had to have some education, typically at Oxford or Cambridge.

By Austen's time, many "livings"—a clergyman's income and position—were controlled by major landholders who could award them to friends and relations. A clergyman could hold more than one living at a time, since he could have more than one patron, or he could even purchase one or more livings. Those patrons who controlled a living would

a rector. Of the two brothers, James was more serious about his duties as a representative of the Church. He had always been a good writer and felt strongly about helping others be their best selves. Henry didn't feel a strong calling to the Church; in spite of various plans, he didn't actually become a clergyman until age forty-six. His religiosity did not run deep—but Austen had enough beloved clergymen in her life to justify trying a new, more respectful approach to men of the cloth.

Creating an angel

Jane Austen's many innovations in *Mansfield Park* often go unrecognized because many readers just don't like Fanny Price, the most proper heroine Austen ever produced. This is one of Austen's other innovative projects in the novel, to produce a nearly angelic heroine full of delicacy and good judgment who does not need to face her faults and improve herself as other Austen characters like Elizabeth Bennet or Emma Woodhouse do. Fanny encounters unpleasant characters in the novel and situations that challenge her sense of decorum and moral virtue, but she conquers all. With Fanny's victory, Austen presents another message to her readers: by being consistently patient, passive, and good, a woman can rise above difficult circumstances. This is not what we expect from Jane Austen; we're a bit startled to see her create a character as proper as Fanny, who won't even act in a private play in her own house when Tom Bertram organizes one and all the others go along (even Edmund). Austen herself grew up in a family dominated by boys and male boarders who loved to put on theatricals; plays put on in the parlor were not new to Austen, and her father the rector allowed them. Austen also wrote the *Juvenilia* when she was quite young, short stories and poems that are full of scandalous events and poorly-behaving women.

> *Fanny Price just doesn't seem to reflect the Jane Austen who had already created Marianne Dashwood, Elizabeth Bennet, and Catherine Morland.*

The influential critic of the 1950s Lionel Trilling calls *Mansfield Park* "a great novel," but he acknowledges that it lacks Austen's usual irony; he also admits that "[t]here is scarcely one of our modern pieties that it does not offend." Certainly Fanny does manage to annoy us modern readers repeatedly. She is no rebel against any sort of social authority, and we love rebels these days. We also love a bad boy who is mostly good (think Han Solo or Captain Jack Sparrow), so Fanny's rejection of the almost entirely good Henry Crawford just seems too priggish to bear. And modern readers generally love a strong, outspoken character, one who won't allow herself to be trampled

present a candidate for religious office to the bishop of the diocese to become a member of the clergy. The diocese had to approve of the candidate—they usually did—and there was a minor ceremony involved; this process is called "taking orders." For those who are interested, check out Daniel Pool's fine explanation of all this in *What Jane Austen Ate and Charles Dickens Knew*.

In *Mansfield Park*, Sir Thomas is a patron with control over two livings, at Mansfield Park and in the nearby town of Thornton Lacey; he first gives the Mansfield Park living to Mr. Norris, then to Mr. Grant. He awards the Thornton Lacey living to his son Edmund— after the bishop in the area approves. Later in the book Edmund takes over the Mansfield Park living, keeping it all in the family.

Photograph of Chawton Church, circa 1871. It has changed little; this is how the exterior would have looked to Jane Austen. Not long after this photo was taken, a fire destroyed part of the nave, which had to be rebuilt.

Everyone Loves a Bad Boy

THE FACT THAT FANNY Price is not popular with many readers demonstrates how difficult it is to create a perfect character whom readers or viewers will like. Samuel Richardson, one of Austen's favorite writers, discovered this himself. His 1748 novel *Clarissa* is often called the longest novel in the English Language: it runs to 1,800 pages in some unabridged editions. Richardson tries to paint his title character as angelically as possible and his villain, the libertine Robert Lovelace, as viciously as possible. But readers were still intrigued with Lovelace—they tended to be more interested in him than in the perfect Clarissa. Richardson revised his novel several times, adding several hundred additional pages and more villainy by Lovelace—and readers were still more fascinated by him than repelled.

The full title of *Clarissa*, by the way, is the following: *Clarissa; or, The History of a Young Lady. Comprehending the Most Important Concerns of Private Life. And Particularly Shewing the Distresses that May Attend the Misconduct Both of Parents and Children in Relation to Marriage.* Light reading for the beach it is not.

by others. So when Fanny silently endures the assaults of the vicious Mrs. Norris, we sympathize with her, but it's hard to like her. "Stand up for yourself," we modern readers say—and so might Elizabeth Bennet and Catherine Morland.

Trilling goes on to say that *Mansfield Park* "seems to controvert everything that [*Pride and Prejudice*] tells us about life," adding that *Mansfield Park*'s "impulse is not to forgive but to condemn. Its praise is not for social freedom but for social stasis." With this Trilling means that no boats are rocked in *Mansfield Park*. The estate will stay firmly in the hands of the Bertrams, the two livings in the hands of good Edmund—he and his cousin and wife Fanny will have good little children who will likely grow up very much like their parents. And no one is forgiven in the novel.

> *Whereas Elizabeth Bennet and Fitzwilliam Darcy forgive each other for their hasty preconceptions and the Bennets come to forgive and accept Wickham to some degree in* Pride and Prejudice, Mansfield Park *doesn't offer a shred of sympathy for Henry Crawford or Maria Bertram Rushworth—both end up miserable and ostracized.*

A minister at last

So why does Trilling think this is a great novel? Well, after acknowledging that nobody "has ever found it possible to like the heroine of *Mansfield Park*," Trilling tells us that Fanny enables Edmund to do what he wants and needs to do: become an ordained minister. Trilling points out that Austen herself said that *Mansfield Park* is about ordination. He asserts that the tension between Fanny and the London-born Mary Crawford, who both want to marry Edmund, "is over what will happen to Edmund as a person, as a man, if he chooses to become a clergyman." Fanny approves of this as a future for Edmund, but Mary does not—she would much rather see him inherit the Bertram estate somehow, or at least become a fine military fellow—something more exciting than a country parson. In the end, Edmund's marriage to Fanny allows him to be what he must be. There's a grand moral achievement at work here, Trilling believes, a victory over appearance and style.

The problem with good girls

The idea that *Mansfield Park* is really about Edmund's choice to become a minister might lessen the guilt of those many readers over the years who could never bring themselves to like shy, passive Fanny.

Given the sensibilities and expectations of Austen's world and later of the Victorians, Fanny should have been a hit, but for well over a hundred years, most of Austen's readers yawned over Mansfield Park.

And many readers still yawn over it. Fanny simply does not translate to the modern world well. Our culture does not like a "goody-two-shoes," and Fanny defines the term. That she won't even participate in a play in her own household entirely mystifies us today; even for those who understand the expectations of the early nineteenth-century woman, it still seems a bit much.

What a difference a generation makes

Fanny does have at least one thing in common with many Austen heroines: like the Bennet and Dashwood sisters, she is caught in a vulnerable situation beyond her own control because she is poor. *Mansfield Park* commences with a description of how the three Ward sisters become settled into marriage and the consequences of the marriages. The sisters belong to a gentry family, and the handsome Maria Ward

Fanny cuts roses out in the sun while her aunt Lady Bertram sits in the shade. 1908 illustration by C. E. Brock.

A young Fanny tolerates her hardhearted aunt, Mrs. Norris. Illustration by Hugh Thomson, circa 1880, from an early edition of *Mansfield Park*.

marries up: she captures the attention of the rich baronet Sir Thomas Bertram and becomes mistress of Mansfield Park. Another Miss Ward—we never find out her first name—marries Mr. Norris, a friend of Sir Thomas's who is a rector (the rather indifferent type); she becomes Mrs. Norris and lives in the parsonage at Mansfield Park after Sir Thomas gives Mr. Norris a living there.

The third Ward sister does not marry well, as Austen tells us:

> *"Miss Frances married, in the common phrase, to disoblige her family, and by fixing on a Lieutenant of Marines, without education, fortune, or connections, did it very thoroughly."*

Frances and her husband, Mr. Price, end up living in Portsmouth, a busy, noisy port city. The fine sisters at Mansfield Park cannot forgive such a deliberate step downward in the socioeconomic hierarchy, so they ignore their sister for many years. Mrs. Price has many children with her husband the Marine, and then he becomes disabled and something of an alcoholic. During her ninth pregnancy, Mrs. Price writes Lady Bertram asking for help. Mrs. Norris takes up the case and brings nine-year-old Fanny Price to Mansfield Park. But

Fanny is treated as a poor relation from her arrival onward; Mrs. Norris, who has a veneer of decorum but behaves hatefully, makes certain that Fanny never forgets her place.

Sir Thomas, a cold and formal man, makes it clear from the beginning that Fanny should always feel the distinction between herself and his own children, saying:

Mrs. Norris, who has a veneer of decorum but behaves hatefully, makes certain that Fanny never forgets her place.

"'There will be some difficulty in our way, Mrs. Norris . . . as to the distinction proper to be made between the girls as they grow up; how to preserve in the minds of my daughters the consciousness of what they are, without making them think too lowly of their cousin; and how, without depressing her spirits too far, to make her remember that she is not a *Miss Bertram*. I should wish to see them very good friends, and would, on no account, authorize in my girls the smallest degree of arrogance towards their relation; but still they cannot be equals.'"

There's a telling message embedded here. The mothers of these girls—of Maria and Julia Bertram and Fanny Price—are sisters who were equals in every way when young. But their culture accepts that one generation of living in different circumstances will create permanent differences in the character of the

Given that Austen chooses to open with the three Ward sisters' equal beginnings, she clearly wants us to notice the unfairness of this sharp distinction between their children.

cousins. The Bertram girls have more merit than Fanny Price, simply because their father has more money and property, and Fanny must know that she is their inferior. Given that Austen chooses to open with the three Ward sisters' equal beginnings, she clearly wants us to notice the unfairness of this sharp distinction between their children.

Predictably enough, young Fanny is miserable at the fine new house. She misses her large family, especially her beloved older brother William. Lady Bertram is indolent and apathetic, no comfort at all; the Bertram girls Maria and Julia at first treat her contemptuously, and her Aunt Norris is a mean-spirited shrew who takes a decided dislike to Fanny upon her arrival. We readers never learn why Mrs. Norris so dislikes Fanny, but there is nothing funny about her treatment of her niece. The other ridiculous and pompous characters of Austen's fictional world are enjoyable—we like laughing at them. But then we don't see *Pride and Prejudice*'s Lady Catherine de Bourgh or *Emma*'s Mrs. Elton emotionally abusing a child or belittling a young woman; they are mostly harmless in the end. In contrast, Mrs. Norris purposefully oppresses Fanny and tries to cut short any promise she shows. The character of Mrs. Norris explains in part why this book isn't as popular as Austen's other works: few readers want to spend much time with her.

Readers of J. K. Rowling's Harry Potter series will recognize the name "Mrs. Norris"—in the Potter tales, she is the nasty, sneaky cat of Hogwarts' caretaker Argus Filch, who likes ruining children's fun just as much as Jane Austen's Mrs. Norris does.

Fanny's reluctance to participate in the play is justified when Sir Thomas returns unexpectedly and catches the others in what he sees as an immodest amusement. Illustration by Hugh Thompson, 1894.

Edmund's kindness

Cousin Edmund, the younger son of Sir Thomas and Lady Bertram, comes to Fanny's rescue. He is several years older than she and helps her write to her

> *At least some of the family fortune arises from slave labor in the New World. This gets little mention in the novel, but it is vital to various interpretations.*

brother William; he continues to comfort her over the ensuing years.

Edmund is kind and dedicated. His ethical dimensions run deep and true; from childhood forward, he deserves the reader's respect.

Not so with Tom Bertram, the eldest child and heir of Mansfield Park. He is self-consumed and shallow, thinking of only his own enjoyment. As he moves into adulthood, he acquires debts through gambling and horse racing that cause the family financial distress. It seems wrong that he will one day control Mansfield Park, when Edmund would run the estate much more effectively—and here we find another example of Austen criticizing her society's system of inheritance.

So Fanny moves into her new life, with one ally and an array of challenging relatives before her. As an Austen protagonist, she's equal to the challenge and grows into an intelligent, perceptive, modest young woman who becomes more indispensable to the lazy Lady Bertram than her two daughters.

The question of slavery

When the Mansfield young people are all in their late teens or early twenties and starting to look for love, Sir Thomas goes to the West Indies to see to his financial concerns there; he takes his debt-ridden son Tom with him. The Bertrams own property in Antigua, including slaves: thus, at least some of the family fortune arises from slave labor in the New World. This gets little mention in the novel, but it is vital to various contemporary interpretations. Edward Said, who has written extensively on materialism and empires, considers *Mansfield Park* the Austen novel that most openly supports the values of the growing British Empire, with Sir Thomas as a maintainer of "the imperial estate," stepping in and straightening things out at home and abroad. But more recently, critic Gabrielle D. V. White has

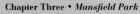

interpreted *Mansfield Park* as undermining support for slavery.

Austen's favorite authors included William Cowper, Samuel Johnson, and Thomas Clarkson, all three of whom were staunchly opposed to slavery.

One of Austen's seafaring brothers was also an abolitionist. White points out that though the Bertrams have a plantation in Antigua, in the novel "there is no endorsement of Sir Thomas's previous handling of his overseas affairs; there is no sign of unwitting testimony of approval of the plantation involvement."

Complicated flirtations

What Sir Thomas is dealing with in Antigua is less important to the action in the novel than the fact that he is gone and the young people have essentially no supervision. While he and Tom are away, Edmund, Maria, Julia, and Fanny meet the charming brother and sister Henry and Mary Crawford. They have come to stay at the Mansfield Park parsonage: their sister Mrs. Grant is married to Mr. Grant, the new rector. Henry and Mary are

Fanny's cousin Edmund comes to her rescue. Woodcut by Joan Hassall, circa 1940s.

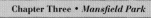

fashionable London types who nonetheless enjoy the country life and the Mansfield young people. Maria and Julia both quickly fall in love with Henry; he flirts with them both, but in the end prefers Maria. This causes a problem, because Maria is by this time engaged to Mr. Rushworth, a very rich but dull and incompetent man. Their wedding will take place as soon as Sir Thomas returns from the West Indies.

Much to Fanny's deep unhappiness, since she is by now in love with her kind cousin, Edmund is drawn to the lovely Mary Crawford.

We twenty-first-century readers of the Western world might think it odd that first cousins would fall in love with each other, but marriages between first cousins were common in Jane Austen's era and before. Austen's favorite brother Henry married their first cousin, Eliza de Feuillide.

Mary is also interested in Edmund, but not his intended profession; she is disappointed to hear that he will take orders and become a rector after his father returns, since the clergy is pretty dull in her opinion—and less flashy than the military, another option for second sons. In spite of this, the attraction between Edmund and Mary grows.

Miniature portrait of Eliza de Feuillide Austen, Jane's cousin; Eliza served as an inspiration for the character of Mary Crawford.

The play's the thing

Tom Bertram returns to Mansfield Park before his father does, and brings his fun-loving friend Mr. Yates with him. The eight young people at Mansfield are without a keeper, as Lady Bertram likely wouldn't notice if the roof collapsed on her and Mrs. Norris won't go against anyone's wishes but Fanny's. Edmund would mind the Mansfield gang well, but once his older brother is there, he cannot: Tom is heir and can do as he pleases. What he pleases to do is put on a play, and the young people approve of the idea, except for Fanny and Edmund, who think it immodest for women to act. Fanny is put into a bad position in regard to the play: her two cousins Maria and Julia don't see the indelicacy in acting. Fanny is convinced that it's deeply wrong, but in saying so, she would be insulting her cousins' propriety. So when pressed by Tom to join them in the play, she responds vaguely but firmly: "'No, indeed, Mr. Bertram, you must excuse me. You cannot have an idea. It would be absolutely impossible for me. If I were to undertake it, I should only disappoint you.'"

This refusal prompts Mrs. Norris to tell Fanny that she is "quite ashamed" of her and to label her "'very ungrateful indeed, considering who and what she is.'"

Such a harsh and humiliating reprimand, delivered before the family and houseguests, prompts astonishment

from Mary and sets her up for her finest moment: she comes to Fanny and sits down next to her, comforting her and smoothing over Mrs. Norris's ugly comments. Edmund becomes all the more smitten with Mary, so much so that he overlooks his objections to the play and joins the production. He says he wants to avoid bringing in an outsider to play the extra male part, but he also wants to act a love scene with Mary Crawford.

Fanny watches and helps and would be involved in the play if she didn't deem it so improper. But the show does not go on after all: Sir Thomas returns earlier than expected and puts an end to the play. The Crawfords and Mr. Yates leave quickly. Sans Henry Crawford, Maria marries her dull but rich Mr. Rushworth, and Julia goes along with Maria on her honeymoon. Tom also leaves for London.

Mr. Crawford's conversion

When the storm over the play has died down and the Bertram sisters are safely gone, Mr. Crawford returns to Mansfield Park and takes a shine to meek Fanny. She, however, has seen the way he toyed with Julia and Maria's affections in front of Maria's fiancé and wants nothing to do with him.

To make Fanny think better of him, Henry helps her brother William, by then a sailor in the British Navy, obtain an officer's commission. While getting

Developing Mary

SOME INSPIRATION FOR the character of Mary Crawford came from Jane Austen's cousin Eliza de Feuillide Austen. Born Elizabeth Hancock in 1761, Eliza was Jane Austen's first cousin: Jane's father's sister's daughter. She was beautiful, flirtatious, and worldly. Born in the British colony of India, she married a French nobleman named Feuillide, who died on a French guillotine in 1794 during the French Revolution. Long before his death, though, Eliza visited the Austens several times without her husband. In 1787-88, she acted in several plays put on by the Austen boys—and both James and Henry fell in love, even though Eliza was older, married, and a mother. It didn't matter—she was fascinating. After her French husband lost his head, Henry proposed to her. She refused him. Then James proposed to her, and she refused him as well. But some time later, Henry tried again and she accepted. Henry, who had planned to go into the clergy, changed his mind after falling for Eliza, perhaps because of her, and became an officer in the military. Like Mary Crawford in *Mansfield Park*, Eliza wasn't keen on the clergy. But Jane Austen doesn't give Mary Crawford the influence that her cousin may have had over her brother: in the novel, Edmund resolutely becomes the minister he was born to be.

to know William better, Henry briefly recognizes that William's character is stronger than his own. This scene in the novel, easily overlooked, is important: it reveals Austen's respect for those who made their fortunes through hard work rather than inheritance—it also foreshadows her creation of Captain Frederick Wentworth in *Persuasion*.

Henry's thoughts convey Austen's growing respect for the man who doesn't merely inherit a comfortable home, income, and lifestyle.

> "The glory of heroism, of usefulness, of exertion, of endurance, made his own habits of selfish indulgence appear in shameful contrast; and he wished he had been a William Price, distinguishing himself and working his way to fortune and consequence with so much self-respect and happy ardour, instead of what he was!"

Henry quickly gets over his longing for a challenging life aboard a ship, but his awareness that William has done something of far more value than he has is telling—it conveys Austen's growing respect for the man who doesn't merely inherit a comfortable home, income, and lifestyle.

As he grows serious in his feelings for Fanny, Henry does show signs of character improvement; he asks her to marry him, despite the difference between them socially. She refuses, in part because of her love for Edmund, but also because of her suspicions that Henry is insincere. Her refusal angers Sir Thomas, who thinks it selfish and unwise of her, but she finds it impossible to tell him why she can't marry a cad like Henry, because the truth reflects badly on his daughters. They did, after all, cheerfully encourage his open flirtation. Sir Thomas sends Fanny back to her impoverished family in Portsmouth for a long visit so she can see what she has come from and how much a rich husband might do for her poor relations. Henry, who appears to develop some real feelings for Fanny, goes to Portsmouth to see her and meet her family, but she still refuses his affection. Rejected, he returns to London, bumps into Maria Bertram Rushworth again, and they run off together. So Henry Crawford is a rake after all, as Fanny always suspected, or so we are to believe.

Fanny, having been sent back to Portsmouth, walks with Henry Crawford along the rampart there. Woodcut by Joan Hassall, circa 1940s.

Scandal in the family

An elegant Fanny Price, looking a little less naïve, at Mansfield Park with her cousin Edmund in the background, 1964.

While Fanny is away from Mansfield Park, everything goes awry for the Bertram family, as she learns through letters. Tom takes a bad fall while drunk and falls into a stupor that nearly kills him. Soon after dealing with this crisis, Sir Thomas and Lady Bertram learn that their married daughter Maria Rushworth has left her home. When Henry Crawford returns to London, he doesn't sit idle. He sees Mrs. Rushworth often, who is unhappy with her husband. They run off together, and then Julia elopes with Mr. Yates to Scotland.

With such bad behavior in young women from such an important household, Austen demonstrates that character has little to do with high birth. These children of a baronet act more wrongly than any other set of siblings in Austen's fiction. For a married woman to leave her husband for another man was about the most scandalous thing a woman could do in 1814. Society also considered it disgraceful if a young woman eloped. Though drunkards and extravagant spenders such as Tom Bertram were more common than erring ladies, such behavior in men still raised eyebrows. That Fanny and William, children of a poor man and a disowned sister, behave so well in contrast to the children of a baronet conveys Austen's growing disillusionment with inherited success.

With seventy-five percent of the Bertram offspring behaving poorly, Edmund comes to Portsmouth to bring Fanny back to Mansfield Park to help support the household. She goes, taking her younger sister Susan with her. Once Edmund and Fanny are home at Mansfield, Mary Crawford reveals herself once and for all to be too much the worldly woman for Edmund and he loses interest in her. Soon after that, Edmund sees that he actually loves Fanny, who still loves him, of course, and they marry.

Everyone loves a bad girl

We know that Fanny and Edmund will be perfect for each other, but this isn't enough to make every reader relate to them.

> In a famously harsh dismissal of the novel and its protagonists, the author Kingsley Amis writes that "to invite Mr. and Mrs. Edmund Bertram round for the evening would not be lightly undertaken." Ouch.

Perhaps Austen wasn't aware of how difficult it is to create a truly good character who keeps one's attention. Perhaps that's why she tries to get us to dislike the likeable brother and sister Henry and Mary Crawford, who, we are supposed to believe, have questionable values. But the two of them have kind impulses as well

as good looks and charm. Mary comforts Fanny after Mrs. Norris chastises her, and later calls her inside when Mrs. Norris sends her on an errand in the rain. She also supports her brother Henry's decision to marry Fanny, who is penniless and beneath him socially. Compare this to the Bingley sisters in *Pride and Prejudice*, who sabotage Jane Bennet when their brother

> *With such bad behavior in young women from such an important household, Austen demonstrates that character has little to do with high birth.*

is drawn to her. Mary simply has far more in common with the expectations of a mainstream woman today than does Fanny Price. Mary Crawford's comments remind us of the playful Elizabeth Bennet as she banters lightheartedly, putting the upright Edmund off balance.

Yes, Mary does rather crassly comment on the good fortune that might come Edmund's way if Tom dies. But let's be honest here: she says out loud what a number of people in the Mansfield area must have been thinking. If the bad Bertram son (Tom) dies, the good Bertram son (Edmund) will get control of the estate. So when Mary jokes that "'I have never bribed a physician in my life'"—to undermine Tom's recovery, she means—we forgive her, even if Fanny doesn't. When Mary says, "'I put it to your conscience, whether

off with another man as particularly wrong or upsetting. "Oh well," we'd think, "so much for that wedding present." Would her reputation be tarnished forever with us? Of course not. But this view of Mary's turns Edmund away from her and toward Fanny at last.

A shift in values

As for Henry Crawford, he has the open-mindedness to propose to Fanny, who is markedly his financial and social inferior—he's certainly not a snob. Henry also helps William move forward in life. Granted, he does this because of Fanny, but it's a nice effort, and he isn't repulsed by the reduced circumstances of Fanny's family when he meets them in Portsmouth. Okay, he is vain and he seems to love Fanny primarily because she's unattainable, but he's not the first to act that way. And his early flirtations with the Bertram sisters that Fanny so condemns? Such flirtation would seem entirely innocent today. Yes, Henry seduces Maria Rushworth—but today if we ostracized women who leave their marriages or men who have affairs with married women, we wouldn't be able to speak to many of those around us. We do have an entirely different social code in the new millennium than existed in Austen's time, but even acknowledging this, it's difficult to dislike Mary or Henry as bad people.

> *The "faults" of Henry and Mary Crawford aren't a big deal anymore, because we've loosened up about sexuality.*

'Sir Edmund' would not do more good with all the Bertram property, than any other possible 'Sir,'" we know that Mary is merely articulating what many of us would think in that situation.

Mary's greatest failing in Edmund's eyes is that she does not think Maria Rushworth's running away with Henry Crawford is particularly bad. She thinks the Mansfield family can cover up the affair easily enough: Rushworth will divorce Maria, and then Henry can marry her. Today we'd think like Mary—we wouldn't see a married woman running

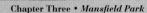

What we learn about ourselves while reading Austen is this: we don't like pompous behavior, hypocrisy, elitism, or selfishness; we don't like flatterers or bullies or lying young men who take advantage of girls or catty women who undermine other women. These are all consistently condemnable behaviors, in Austen's era and our own—so we find Mrs. Norris repulsive. In Austen's other books, we don't like Lady Catherine de Bourgh, Mrs. John Dashwood, General Tilney, Mr. and Mrs. Elton, or Sir Walter Elliot. We despise Mr. Collins and think Mr. Wickham just awful and we loathe the Bingley sisters. The "faults" of Henry and Mary Crawford aren't a big deal anymore, because we've loosened up about sexuality. But arrogance and manipulation? Those are still sins.

In the end, Mary and Henry are just more fun than Fanny and Edmund. They are savvy and sophisticated and good-hearted, and if they choose to live near the edges of the narrow confines of their culture, for the most part we don't blame them—it's a pretty restrictive culture.

Reinterpreting the novel

The 1999 Miramax/BBC film *Mansfield Park* takes a Crawfordesque approach to Austen's novel, playing up the fun aspects of the story with little regard for a strict, faithful interpretation. Mary Crawford,

Henry Crawford (Alessandro Nivola) and Mary Crawford (Embeth Davidtz) playing billiards in the 1999 film adaptation of *Mansfield Park*.

well played by the lovely Embeth Davidtz, becomes a Virginia Slims poster figure, sharing a cigarette with her brother Henry while playing a game of billiards with the guys. Edmund sees nothing amiss in this, even though the year is 1806, not 1926. There are also two highly charged homoerotic scenes between Mary and Fanny, instigated by Mary. The scenes are

Fanny also accepts Henry Crawford's marriage proposal in the film—echoing Jane Austen's overnight engagement to Harris Bigg-Wither.

tastefully done and appealing, given the exquisite beauty of the two actresses. But lesbian love in Jane Austen's *Mansfield Park*? On what page? Given how straitlaced Fanny is in the book and the era the novel was written, such scenes just don't fit.

In the hands of director and screenplay writer Patricia Rozema, Fanny Price (Frances O'Connor) becomes a hybridized form of Jane Austen herself, Fanny Price, abolitionist Harriet Beecher Stowe,

and Audrey Hepburn. The screenplay draws from *Mansfield Park* and Austen's *Juvenilia*, as well as Austen's own life, but it also includes such an expansion of any abolitionist message that Austen might have included in the novel that the film becomes difficult to embrace as Austenian.

> *This film more than any other recent one conveys our modern desire to shape Austen to meet our own culture's expectations, to make her into a cosmopolitan multicultural writer so that we can enjoy her writing without being bothered by her privileged position in the British gentry.*

The film also reflects our world's general disregard of history. Rozema's *Mansfield Park* so contorts the basic story that it almost feels like a parody of Austen and what we know of her era.

Tom Bertram is a drunken teenager when were first see him. Later we find that he's a drunk for a reason: he is so distraught that his family makes their money from slave labor that he can't function without alcohol. We learn what a tortured, sensitive soul Tom is when he returns from Antigua with sketches that he drew of his father Sir Thomas raping female slaves and of slave tortures on the plantation; Sir Thomas catches Fanny looking at the drawings and yells uncontrollably at her. Of course, Austen writes nothing of this in *Mansfield Park*, but it makes for high drama to include such scenes in the film.

The film version of Fanny Price's character just doesn't work. Meek Fanny runs and skips with Edmund at the beginning of the film, in full view of anyone in the household, and she boldly asks Sir Thomas about the slave trade in the movie. In the book we don't know how Fanny asks about the slave trade, as she brings it up with Edmund after the fact. But the characters in the film see nothing schizophrenic in passive Fanny suddenly asking her stern uncle provocative questions. A much less proper Fanny also is highly sexual and drunk at the ball Sir Thomas puts on for her. And a fickle Fanny also accepts Henry Crawford's marriage proposal, though she changes her mind the next day—echoing Jane Austen's overnight engagement to Harris Bigg-Wither. Fanny enjoys a kiss with Henry—and it's far more sexual than the one she later shares with Edmund.

Rozema tries to do too much with her version of *Mansfield Park*; Jane Austen and Fanny Price and a sexualized abolitionist just can't fit into the same character. But with a difficult heroine like Fanny Price, *Mansfield Park* may never have made it to the big screen any other way.

Frances O'Connor as Fanny in the 1999 film adaptation. Three actresses play Fanny at different ages in the film.

Chapter Three • *Mansfield Park*

Chapter Four

EMMA

"Seldom, very seldom, does complete truth belong to any
human disclosure; seldom can it happen that something is
not a little disguised, or a little mistaken…"

In January 1814, when Jane Austen

sat down to write *Emma*, two of her books had been published (*Sense and Sensibility* and *Pride and Prejudice*) and another one was on the way (*Mansfield Park*). Austen didn't make herself rich or famous with her writing, but she had established herself as a talented writer. Perhaps that is why she writes of someone new: a young woman in a position of privilege. Emma Woodhouse is the only one of Austen's protagonists who is rich and well-connected.

Austen did not write *Emma* from experience. Despite the success of her books, her life had not changed materially; she still lived with her mother and sister in her brother Edward's cottage at Chawton. She still wrote in the sitting room, and she still wrote anonymously, though the family did not try to hide Austen's identity as an author any longer.

Emma was published in late 1815, and Emma herself is one of Austen's most successful and likeable characters. She is also a less savvy protagonist, akin to Catherine Morland of *Northanger Abbey* in her hasty, silly assumptions. She lacks the self-awareness that the Dashwood sisters, the elder Bennet sisters, Fanny Price, Anne Elliot, and Catherine Morland all have to some extent. But never mind. We love Emma. We like watching her grow up, we like watching her essential generosity emerge, we like watching her

Watercolor by Cassandra Austen depicting Fanny Austen-Knight. Fanny, perhaps Jane Austen's favorite niece, was the eldest daughter of Jane's wealthy brother Edward.

The Attentions of a Prince

AUSTEN DISCOVERED IN 1815 that the Prince Regent of Britain was one of her most devoted fans, and that he had a set of her books at each of his residences. Her nephew James Edward Austen-Leigh writes in his biography of Austen that she went to visit the Prince's personal librarian while in London. The librarian, acting on behalf of the Prince, invited her to dedicate a book to the Prince, and so the dedication page of *Emma* reads like this: "To His Royal Highness the Prince Regent, this work is, by His Royal Highness's permission, most respectfully dedicated, by His Royal Highness's dutiful and obedient humble servant, The Author." Some say the wording has a bit of her famous irony in it—it does seem a little over the top. But in any case, to have drawn the notice of one of the most powerful men in the world was an achievement.

The Prince Regent, later King George IV, in his Garter Robes, by Sir Thomas Lawrence, 1816.

win the grandest man in the area. And we might even like watching Austen's richest heroine make some humiliating and leveling mistakes.

Emma's experiment

The novel is an intersecting maze of hidden schemes and potential couples. The central plotline follows Emma Woodhouse as she conducts an egalitarian experiment: she befriends a penniless girl with low prospects to bring her into her society and find her a well-off husband. Emma herself never has to worry about money. She is the second of two daughters of the rich Mr. Woodhouse, owner of Hartfield, the central estate of the village of Highbury, where the Woodhouses are "first in consequence." Perhaps because of Emma's privileged position, or because she doesn't fully understand her culture's rules yet—or a combination of these—she thinks that certain truths about her society don't apply to her. She will learn differently.

Emma embraces as her friend Miss Harriet Smith, "the natural daughter of nobody knows whom." This meant that Harriet's parents were not legally married at the time of her birth. If a man had the integrity and the money to do so, he would support such a daughter, as Harriet's father does by paying for her enrollment at Mrs. Goddard's school. Harriet would be considered "illegitimate" all her life, as it was considered a social disgrace not to come from a sanctioned marriage. But

Emma overlooks this in Harriet's case. Her experiment is not exactly a revolution, though: she is interested in lifting only Harriet up to a higher social level. She has no interest in the many other disadvantaged people of her area.

> *The narrow nature of Emma's experiment suggests its true intent: to see if she can do something attention-getting, something that breaks her culture's rules. Pretty typical for a twenty-year-old.*

Flush with the success of having arranged (or so she believes) the match between her former governess Miss Taylor and her neighbor Mr. Weston, Emma forges ahead. As a first step, she convinces Harriet to reject the farmer Robert Martin's marriage proposal. Harriet is flattered by Emma's attention and follows her lead. Emma then tries to match Harriet with Mr. Elton, the well-off local clergyman of Hartfield. He stands several steps higher on the socioeconomic ladder than Mr. Martin and Harriet, and he thinks highly of himself.

> *Emma fails to see that Mr. Elton, a self-promoter and selfish man, intends himself for her, Emma Woodhouse, the richest woman in the area.*

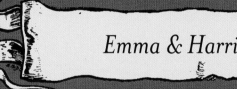

Emma & Harriet as Equals on Film

IN THE 1996 MIRAMAX film *Emma*, director Douglas McGrath presents Emma as having real democratic impulses at first. Once again, this is an attempt to update a character and plot to meet our contemporary expectations. Emma can be a genuinely unfeeling snob in the beginning of Austen's novel. McGrath mutes this trait in Emma and emphasizes her effort to raise up someone who is less fortunate than she. We see this in the framing of a shot as Harriet and Emma sit before the fire; they sit opposite one another, neither sitting above or below the other, apparently equals. In one scene, when Emma admits to Harriet her folly about Mr. Elton, that he actually wants to marry the rich Miss Woodhouse, she places her head in Harriet's lap, saying that Harriet is a far better person than she. Later, in front of that same fire with the same egalitarian setting, we see Harriet throw her head into Emma's lap, wondering how she shall ever get over Mr. Martin. In that room, the two are equals—until Mr. Knightley inadvertently divides them and ends Emma's social experiment.

Gwyneth Paltrow as Emma in the 1996 film adaptation, directed by Douglas McGrath.

Austen in Beverly Hills

MORE THAN ANY OF the other movies based on books by Jane Austen, Amy Heckerling's *Clueless* (1995) conveys Austen's timelessness; the film also shows the English-speaking world's tendency to rediscover Austen generation after generation. The lighthearted film takes place in Beverly Hills, with a plot straight from *Emma*. The modern Emma, rich girl Cher (Alicia Silverstone), is vain and manipulative; as in the novel, she overcomes this. Her reward is Josh, her older ex-stepbrother, whom at first she dismisses but eventually comes to love.

Cher's experiment sticks close to the novel: she adopts Tai, an underdressed new girl, gives her a makeover, and talks her out of dating the friendly "burnout" Travis. She also, of course, tries to set Tai up with a guy of higher social standing. We know what happens. The arrogant Elton is never interested in Tai; he likes Cher all along. Tai eventually finds happiness with Travis, Elton gets what he deserves with the irritating Amber, and Cher ends up with her Josh. Other details match up as well—like Cher's devotion to her father's health—and can be fun to spot.

In the end, Cher does the right thing: she learns to care for others more and think of herself less. No one gets married, though. As if—they *are* in high school.

After several months of machinations to marry Mr. Elton to Miss Smith, Emma must, with great humiliation over not seeing Mr. Elton's real intentions, reject his marriage proposal on a snowy Christmas Eve.

A failed matchmaker

But Emma has not learned a lesson yet. She still hopes to find Harriet a wealthy man and improve her place in Hartfield society, so she focuses on Mr. Frank Churchill, who will inherit a large estate. But Emma misunderstands that Harriet is not quietly in love with Mr. Churchill but in love with Mr. Knightley, a neighbor of the Woodhouses and the most wealthy and powerful man in the area. Emma also does not know that Mr. Churchill is already secretly engaged to the talented and penniless Jane Fairfax. Unaware and undaunted, Emma forges on, attending strawberry pickings and picnics, enjoying herself while assuming she knows exactly what is going on.

The wisdom of Mr. Knightley

Mr. Knightley understands their culture far better than Emma does, and often tries to caution her that she does not understand matters as well as

she thinks. But he is thirty-seven (or thirty-eight) and Emma is twenty; therefore, she feels certain that Mr. Knightley is just plain wrong. But Mr. Knightley repeatedly proves he has greater insight than Emma. From their first gentle dispute about whether she made Mrs. Weston's lucky marriage possible to more serious arguments about Robert Martin's proposal to Harriet, Mr. Elton's intentions, Frank Churchill's relationship to Jane Fairfax, and her own treatment of Miss Bates, Mr. Knightley continually trumps Emma by being right. Austen portrays this man who holds so much power over tenants and others in the area as deserving his influence.

> *Mr. Knightley is one of the few very rich characters that Austen presents favorably, even, in this case, faultlessly.*

Also as part of her experiment, Emma tries on the possibility of remaining a single rich woman. But over the course of the novel, she realizes the power of men. The men in the novel have agency, they can make things happen: Mr. Martin can ask Harriet Smith to marry him, whether Emma likes it or not; Mr. Elton can ignore what Emma intends for him and pursue his own self-interest; Mr. Churchill can tease her while hiding his real intentions; and Mr. Knightley may do anything he likes—pick up the Bateses and

Miss Fairfax in his carriage, defend Robert Martin, save a young woman from a prominent man's snub, go to London whenever he pleases, and ask anyone to marry him, even Emma. Emma can do none of these things.

Sorting out the weddings

The novel—and Emma's experiment—ends with all the true loves revealed and everyone falling into their expected social places. Harriet marries Mr. Martin after all, a man of her level (Mr. Knightley would say she sits below Mr. Martin); Mr. Elton marries his Augusta with her ten thousand pounds; and the first woman of the area, our Emma, falls in love with and marries the first man of the area, Mr. Knightley, the brother of her sister's husband. Frank Churchill does save Jane Fairfax from the life of a working girl by marrying her, but as Elizabeth Bennet might observe, Jane is a gentleman's daughter, and Frank is a gentleman; so far they are equals. So though Frank has not improved his economic state by marrying, the social system has not been strained.

Obviously, marriage is the focus of the novel. Couplings are vital among human beings in general, of course, but in Austen's world of the English gentry, romance leads to marriage leads to babies and inheritances. Who marries whom and where the wealth comes from holds the utmost importance. All the couplings prove educational to Emma; by novel's end, she herself wants to be part of the marriage game, with all of its love and babies and allocation of real estate.

Learning the truth about marriage

Emma's shifting view of marriage reveals much about her learning process and her culture itself. Early on, she tells Harriet that she doesn't see the necessity of marriage:

"'I have none of the usual inducements of women to marry. Were I to fall in love, indeed, it would be a different thing! but I never have been in love; it is not my way, or my nature; and I do not think I ever shall. And, without love, I am sure I should be a fool to change such a situation as mine. Fortune I do not want; employment I do not want; consequence I do not want: I believe few married women are half as much mistress of their husband's house, as I am of Hartfield; and never, never could I expect to be so truly beloved and important; so always first and always right in any man's eyes as I am in my father's.'"

ENVELOPE CONTENTS

- *Sketch of Jane Austen* by her sister Cassandra, circa 1810. This is the only certain portrait from Jane's lifetime in existence, reproduced at its actual size. Austen's niece Caroline Austen says this of the portrait: "though the general resemblance is *not* strong, yet as it represents a pleasing countenance it is so far a truth."

- *Watercolor of Jane,* then in her late twenties, painted by her sister Cassandra in 1804.

The White Knight of Donwell Abbey

WHEN ROBERT MARTIN decides he wants to marry Harriet Smith, he goes to Mr. Knightley to discuss his intention to propose to her. Though Mr. Martin is ostensibly asking for guidance, he is also effectively asking his social and economic superior for permission to get married. The kind landlord grants his approval of the match.

Mr. Knightley watches his flock carefully—he wants no one out of step. Hence his frustrations when Emma threatens to upset the social order. Mr. Knightley knows that a Miss Smith, representing "illegitimacy and ignorance" —and far more importantly, having little money and a low social position—cannot marry Mr. Elton, Highbury's clergyman, or an heir like Frank Churchill, without some social upheaval. Mr. Knightley wants things to remain as they are. Given the tumult going on in France that Mr. Knightley (and Jane Austen) has viewed over his life, one can hardly blame him for wanting to keep matters stable in the English countryside. So he disapproves of Emma's friendship with Harriet Smith, as he explains to Mrs. Weston: "And as for Harriet, I will venture to say that *she*

cannot gain by the acquaintance. Hartfield will only put her out of conceit with all the other places she belongs to. She will grow just refined enough to be uncomfortable with those among whom birth and circumstances have placed her home.'"

Mr. Knightley has a strong sense of *noblesse oblige*. He has obligations to his parish and to neighboring Highbury: he is expected to keep order in the area. So he advises tenants. He helps his hypochondriac neighbor Mr. Woodhouse make financial decisions. He gives carriage rides to poor Miss Bates and her "portionless" niece (although he would never go so far as to change the system that has worked against the two unfortunate women). He dances with lowly Harriet after the odious Mr. Elton snubs her. He pays attention to who is courting whom, to quiet intrigues that no one else picks up on. Through his insight and tendency to be right about matters, Austen suggests that the British system works overall. With nearly telepathic men like Mr. Knightley in charge, we need not worry about haves and have-nots, because we are in good hands. His name, of course, is no accident: he is a white knight of the realm.

She also reveals her own ignorance of the vital link between marriage and inheritance. She absorbs her first lesson in regard to marriage and property when she hears of Mrs. Weston's suspicions that Mr. Knightley loves Jane Fairfax. Emma rejects the idea, thinking of six-year-old Henry, her sister Isabella's oldest boy; Isabella has married Mr. John Knightley, Mr. Knightley's younger brother. As things stand, Henry will inherit Donwell Abbey from Mr. Knightley because Mr. Knightley has no son. Aware of this, Emma declares the idea of a match between Knightley and Jane "mad." Mrs. Weston reminds Emma that aside from an "inequality of fortune, and perhaps a little disparity of age," there is nothing unsuitable about Mr. Knightley's marrying Jane Fairfax. Emma responds as follows:

"'But Mr. Knightley does not want to marry. I am sure he has not the least idea of it. Do not put it into his head. Why should he marry?—He is as happy as possible by himself; with his farm, and his sheep, and his library, and all the parish to manage; and he is extremely fond of his brother's children. He has no occasion to marry, either to fill up his time or his heart.'"

The physical release of marriage for men and women who remain chaste until marriage has apparently not yet occurred to Emma as a reason to wed; she hasn't yet considered that Mr. Knightley's farm and his sheep just might not be enough for him. (A crude writer might here point out that perhaps Mr. Knightley has gone so long without marrying because of his relationship with his sheep, but such adolescent observations do not belong in a book about Jane Austen. And to even imagine such a thing about Mr. Knightley!)

Retaining control of the land

Emma also has not considered the property distribution questions that so involve the whole parish. Will the unmarried Mr. Knightley of thirty-seven (or -eight) be satisfied to pass Donwell Abbey on to his nephew? And who will take over Hartfield, given that Mr. Woodhouse has no son? Has this doddering man perhaps entailed his entire estate to some gentleman Emma and the Knightleys do not know about, perhaps Mr. Perry,

Mr. Knightley speaks with Mrs. Bates at her window.
Illustration by C. E. Brock, circa 1895.

the apothecary, whom Mr. Woodhouse so adores? Or did some man irrevocably entail the estate decades before, directing it out of the Woodhouse line if Mr. Woodhouse did not produce a son? Something like this did happen to Mr. Bennet in *Pride and Prejudice*, after all. We are never told such things, nor what will happen to Emma upon her

by herself once her father dies; by law and custom, single women did not inherit big estates.

In *Emma*, everyone who lives in the Highbury area has something at stake in the question of who will inherit Mr. Woodhouse's and Mr. Knightley's property, for the Woodhouses and the Knightleys are the gentry around whom the neighborhood turns.

The physical release of marriage for men and women who remain chaste until marriage has apparently not yet occurred to Emma as a reason to wed.

As was typical of rural counties in nineteenth-century England, the rich landowners in *Emma* control most of the farmland, and the tenants with their small farms depend on the local landowners for the use of their land. The landowners in turn depend on the rent their tenants pay—which the tenants are able to pay because of their labor and their ability to make the land produce. The relationship is a mutual one, even symbiotic—some might also say parasitic, with the landowners as the parasites.

father's death, but we do know that Mr. Knightley wonders about her fate early in the novel. While talking to Mrs. Weston, he observes, "'There is an anxiety, a curiosity in what one feels for Emma. I wonder what will become of her!'" With such a question, the insightful Mr. Knightley suggests that he has considered the Knightley and Woodhouse property matters, even if Emma has not. He likely realizes that she will not be able to stay at Hartfield

In order for this system to remain stable, a landowner had to have an heir so that he could be certain of the future of his property. Frank Churchill, the former Frank Weston, comes into his wealth in part because of his family's concerns about inheritance. The Churchills, Frank's uncle and

The Harvest Field by William Frederick Witherington, depicting workers on an English farm in the mid-1800s.

Godmersham Park, Kent, the home of Edward Austen Knight. Engraving by William Watts, 1785.

Chapter Four • *Emma*

aunt, have no heir and are attached to young Frank. So when the first Mrs. Weston dies, they adopt Frank as their heir. Mr. Weston, who had yet to become comfortable financially, agreed to the arrangement as the best outcome for his motherless son.

Edward Austen becomes a great landowner

Good-luck stories like Frank Churchill's actually happened, as Jane Austen knew well. Her brother Edward benefited from a similar situation, as the adopted heir of a rich couple.

> Edward eventually became the owner of a sizeable estate called Godmersham and married the daughter of a baronet. As a wealthy landowner, he was able to help his family in various ways—for example, he inherited the cottage in Chawton where his mother and two sisters lived for the last years of Jane Austen's life.

Edward Austen was apparently very charming as a boy, which set all these events in motion. At the age of twelve, he caught the eye of the Knights, distant cousins of the Austens, who had just married. They liked him so much they asked that he join them on their honeymoon. Though twenty-first-century readers may find this inexplicable, the Knights and Edward all seem to have had a nice time—and four years later, after no children were born to the Knights, they asked the Austens for permission to adopt Edward as their heir.

Even a single woman who is "handsome, clever, and rich" like Emma has an uncertain future. It is Emma's father who is rich, not Emma.

What will become of Emma?

Inheritance affected women indirectly and through men; women did not stand to inherit much of their own. So the truth is, even a single woman who is "handsome, clever, and rich" like Emma has an uncertain future. It is Emma's father who is rich, not Emma. She lives very comfortably and has everything she could want while feeling no anxiety for herself, but like all of Austen's heroines, much depends upon whom she marries.

Though rich young women of Austen's world were looked on favorably, certain things were expected of them. The very idea that Emma, the richest young lady of the area, would *not* marry is preposterous, for

> *"It darted through her, with the speed of an arrow, that Mr. Knightley must marry no one but herself!"*

she is the potential producer of a high-born male heir. She will not likely inherit a large chunk of land herself, as Hartfield is a small estate. Emma's wealth lies primarily in her dowry, but she needs to marry for that transfer of funds to take place; then the thousands of pounds attached to her will legally become the property of her husband. This is one of the quiet lessons of the novel: Emma learns that the

life of a rich single woman, living alone as she pleases in a large mansion, may not be possible. In all of Austen's works, we do not see one such woman—the rich Lady Catherine, Mrs. Ferrars, Lady Russell, and Mrs. Norris all have their own money, but they are all widows.

Given the inheritance patterns within their social circle, Emma is relieved by Mr. Knightley's assurances that he does not love Jane Fairfax; her concerns about her nephew's inheritance are temporarily eased. But she must later face the facts of inheritance again when she hears that Harriet loves Mr. Knightley and believes him to return her affections. If this is true, Donwell Abbey could end up with the child of an "illegitimate" woman rather than in Henry's lap. This moment may have the same importance for Emma that seeing Pemberley does for Elizabeth Bennet. Emma finally realizes the meaning of marriage and inheritance—and she discovers immediately afterward that she loves Mr. Knightley: "It darted through her, with the speed of an arrow, that Mr. Knightley must marry no one but herself!"

The danger of remaining single

The single women who are left out of the property game in the novel serve as a warning of what might happen to Emma if she remains headstrong enough

A Rake's Progress V: The Rake marrying an Old Woman, by William Hogarth, 1733. Unmarried women were vulnerable all their lives, rich or not: this painting depicts a rich old spinster lured into marriage by an unscrupulous young man.

Frank Churchill displays some subtle affection as he shines Miss Fairfax's glasses for her. Illustration from an early edition of *Emma* by Hugh Thomson, circa 1880.

to believe she never needs to marry. In this novel as in others, Austen portrays the socioeconomic vulnerability of women. The Bates family provides the best example of this. Although Miss Bates's orphaned niece Jane Fairfax is talented, modest, and pretty, none of it matters—it's a governess's life for her, for she has no inheritance. She feels bitter about her fate; at the Woodhouses' dinner party for Mrs. Elton, she has "a quivering lip, a tear in the eye"—in part about her relationship with the absent Mr. Churchill, which she must hide, but also because of the strong possibility that she will soon have to take a job as a governess, even if only until she can marry Mr. Churchill.

Though Jane's fate is uncertain, she wants no help from Mrs. Elton, who forces heavy-handed attentions on her. Jane asks Mrs. Elton not to help her find a position: "'When I am quite determined as to the time, I am not at all afraid of being long unemployed. There are places in town, offices, where inquiry would soon produce something—Offices for the sale—not quite of human flesh—but of human intellect.'" Mrs. Elton quickly assures Jane that her contact Mr. Suckling is in favor of abolishing the slave trade, and Jane replies: "'I was not thinking of the slave-trade,' replied Jane; 'governess trade, I assure you, was all that I had in view; widely different certainly as to the guilt of those who carry it on; but as to the greater misery of the victims, I do not know where it lies.'" That Miss Fairfax would compare the

The Governess by Richard Redgrave, 1844. Governesses occupied a lonely position in society—above the
ordinary household servants but below the family whose children they taught.

life of a paid governess to a slave conveys her naïveté, and Austen's, about the viciousness of slavery throughout the world in 1815.

But the resentful remark on the life of a governess does convey the frustration of the two Janes—Fairfax and Austen—over women's limited

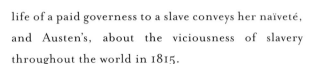
Emma is aware of Miss Bates's unfortunate fate, but talks callously about it early in the novel.

options in Britain in the early nineteenth century: both of them see women as trapped beings who have little agency over their own futures. Jane Fairfax brings this up again as she rushes from the outing at Donwell Abbey, determined to walk home. Emma objects, worried that she should not walk alone to Highbury, but Jane resists, explaining herself: "'Miss Woodhouse, we all know at times what it is to be wearied in spirits. Mine, I confess,

are exhausted. The greatest kindness you can show me, will be to let me have my own way, and only say that I am gone when it is necessary.'" Emma, understanding how infrequently women have their own way, immediately agrees to Jane's request. As they part, Jane conveys the difficulties of living always with others, of being always dependent on others. "'Oh! Miss Woodhouse, the comfort of being sometimes alone!'"

The commentary suggests Jane Austen herself, hiding her writing pages under a blotting sheet when someone entered the room, not allowing the squeaky door to be fixed so she could tell when another interruption was coming. She also wanted to be alone, to pursue her writing without hindrance or judgment.

The insensitivity of privilege

Miss Bates is also a pathetic woman, caught with no clear role in her society. Though unmarried and relatively poor, she never had to become a governess. Still, she lives in reduced circumstances with her mother in an apartment in Highbury; her fate is not a good one, as Mr. Knightley forcefully points out to Emma near the end of the novel. Emma is aware of Miss Bates's unfortunate fate, but talks callously about it early in the novel. Consider

Mr. Knightley shares his wisdom with Emma, in an early edition of the novel. Illustration by Hugh Thomson, circa 1880.

her conversation with Harriet, after she has told her friend that she does not intend to marry:

> "But then, to be an old maid at last, like Miss Bates!" [said Harriet.]
>
> "That is as formidable an image as you could present, Harriet; and if I thought I should ever be like Miss Bates! so silly—so satisfied—so smiling—so prosing—so undistinguished and unfastidious—and

with a very narrow income, must be a ridiculous, disagreeable, old maid! the proper sport of boys and girls; but a single woman, of good fortune, is always respectable . . ."

Emma's comments are cruel, and she seems to have forgotten that her own good friend Mrs. Weston, formerly Miss Taylor and her governess, was "a single woman with a very narrow income" not long before.

Throughout the novel, Emma is oblivious that she is being manipulative, but we love her in spite of her flaws.

Austen herself is also "a poor old maid" as she writes the novel, which reminds the reader that, in this instance, Austen is not on Emma's side; rather, she shows her culture's harsh and limited attitude toward single women via her clueless Emma.

so apt to tell every thing relative to every body about me, I would marry to-morrow. But between us, I am convinced there never can be any likeness, except in being unmarried."

> "But still, you will be an old maid! and that's so dreadful!"
>
> "Never mind, Harriet, I shall not be a poor old maid; and it is poverty only which makes celibacy contemptible to a generous public! A single woman,

A happy ending

In *Emma*, our heroine learns a few lessons about herself and the way her culture works, then willingly steps into the position that her society has reserved for her: the daughter of a rich man marries the benign overlord of the area. Once she becomes Mrs. Knightley, we have no reason to believe that she tries to elevate any more Harriet Smiths or upset the hierarchy she benefits so much from.

> As Austen puts it, "The intimacy between [Harriet] and Emma must sink; their friendship must change into a calmer sort of goodwill; and, fortunately, what ought to be, and must be, seemed already beginning, and in the most gradual, natural manner."

Note the word "natural"—that two friends of different socioeconomic spheres must stop being friends is inevitable in the world view Austen presents here. Emma's experiment is over.

But what would become of Emma if she didn't have Mr. Knightley? Because there is both land and money in her family, her fate would not be as restricted as that of Miss Bates. Likely enough, Hartfield would drop into young Henry's lap. If she did not marry, our Emma would then get to stay on at Hartfield as a maiden aunt—if Henry allowed it. Though nephews did not have to allow such things in 1815, we readers quickly tell ourselves that no nephew could be cruel to an aunt as lovable as Auntie Emma.

Harriett and Mr. Martin speak on the road, as Emma looks on.
Illustration by Hugh Thomson, circa 1880.

Chapter Four • *Emma*

The Objections of Charlotte Brontë

CHARLOTTE BRONTË would never use the words "masterpiece" and "Jane Austen" in the same sentence. She does not like Austen's works; she finds *Pride and Prejudice* tightly confined and has this to say of Austen after reading *Emma*:

" . . . she ruffles her reader by nothing vehement; disturbs him by nothing profound: the Passions are perfectly unknown to her; she rejects even a speaking acquaintance with that stormy Sisterhood; even to the Feelings she vouchsafes no more than an occasional graceful but distant recognition; too frequent converse with them would ruffle the smooth elegance of her progress. . . . Jane Austen was a complete and most sensible lady, but a very incomplete, and rather insensible (not senseless) woman, if this is heresy—I cannot help it."

All three of the Brontë sisters privilege emotion in their works (note the capital-ization of "Passions" and "Feelings" above), including Charlotte Brontë's dark romance, *Jane Eyre*. So her dismissal of Jane Austen is to be expected. Brontë creates a much more obviously rebellious heroine in her title char-acter Jane Eyre and injects far more drama into her works—more *happens* in her plots than does in Austen's novels. The orphan Jane stands up to Mrs. Reed, her aunt by marriage, telling her exactly what she thinks of her and her children, who have all abused her. She also counters Mr. Brocklehurst, the cruel head of the school she is sent to, and later she resists the demanding Mr. Rochester, whom she loves, but he carries quite a bit of baggage with him, legal and otherwise. Brontë's embrace of high drama and passionate responses to that drama is worlds different than Austen's calmer—and more realistic—scenes.

Charlotte Brontë. Oil on canvas portrait by J. H. Thompson, circa mid-1800s.

Throughout the novel, Emma is oblivious that she is being manipulative, but we love her in spite of her flaws. There is, after all, a good impulse at work in Emma—she's trying to help a virtual orphan who has no money and few friends. And Emma does become a better person over the course of the novel. At first condescending and harsh toward Miss Bates, she learns that such treatment of others is unpardonable. She tries to make amends for her behavior and learns to think of others. This is no small feat.

But as a social experimenter Emma fails utterly. Her hypotheses are all wrong. Mr. Elton does not love Harriet—he knows his worth. Mr. Churchill does not love Emma, as Emma imagines he does, and she does not see the relationship between Mr. Churchill and Jane. She even mistakes her own mind, thinking that she loves Mr. Churchill. And she believes Harriet loves Mr. Churchill when she actually loves Mr. Knightley.

On a plot level, Emma's mistakes are amusing, akin to the stumbling antics of a comedy team.

On a romantic level, the reader likes to conjecture about possible couplings, the futures possible with each. And on a class level, the reader enjoys seeing Austen portray once again just how fallible and wrong-headed the rich can be, however lovable a rich young woman can be at the same time. As for the reading experience, the novel is lively, full of engaging and likeable characters—except Mr. Elton and his wife, whom we love to despise.

Sir Walter Scott, himself a famous author, wrote an unsigned 1816 review for the *Quarterly Review* in which he praises Austen's characters as realistic; he declares that Austen "has produced sketches of such spirit and originality." R. W. Chapman of Oxford, the critic who did so much to promote Austen's works, calls *Emma* Austen's "masterpiece."

Perhaps Austen's characterizations work so well because she herself cares about them so much. As James Edward Austen-Leigh tells us of his aunt, Jane Austen "took a kind of parental interest in the beings whom she had created, and did not dismiss them from her thoughts when she had finished the last chapter." Of Emma, Austen herself said, "I am going to take a heroine whom no one but myself will much like." It's sad to have to say this, but Austen was wrong.

An illustration of a woman writing in a morning dress. Published in
Rudolph Ackermann's Repository of Arts, 1822.

Chapter Five

NORTHANGER ABBEY

"Provided that nothing like useful knowledge could be gained from them, provided they were all story and no reflection, she had never any objection to books at all."

In a sense, Jane Austen's first complete writing

is *Northanger Abbey*: it's the first novel she sold to a publisher. But it's complicated: of her six major novels, Austen started *Sense and Sensibility* first—probably in 1795—but she revised it later. She wrote *Pride and Prejudice* second, in 1796-97. Austen's father tried to get that novel published in 1797, but failed, and Austen also overhauled the novel later. Her third book was *Susan*, probably written in 1798-99; she would later change the name of this novel to *Northanger Abbey*. In 1803, while she was living in Bath, she sold *Susan* to a publisher named Richard Crosby in London for ten pounds. The manuscript stalled with Crosby for years, remaining unpublished although he held the rights to it. In 1809 Austen contacted Crosby, asking why he had not published her book. She also tried to get it back from him, but he would only agree to do so if she paid him back the ten pounds he had paid for it. Austen could not afford to spare ten pounds at that point in her life, so the manuscript continued to gather dust. In the spring of 1816, after Austen's other successes and as she was finishing *Persuasion*, her brother Henry purchased the rights to *Susan*; he would publish it as *Northanger Abbey* together with *Persuasion* in December 1817 after Austen's death.

Austen wrote a rather angry notice to her readers after Henry bought back the rights, telling them the book's publication history.

Faraway Thoughts by Charles Cope West, painted in the mid-1800s.

The Youngest Novel

BECAUSE OF NORTH~ anger Abbey's unusual publishing history, it serves as a time capsule of sorts, preserving Austen's early writing style. Though it was published with the last of Austen's novels, *Persuasion*, *Northanger Abbey* is probably the "youngest" of her major works, in that Austen revised it the least. Austen wrote the first drafts of *Sense and Sensibility* and *Pride and Prejudice* before starting to write *Northanger Abbey*, but she revised them extensively when she was older. We don't know what the original draft of *Susan* looked like, but once Austen got it back in 1816, she had little time to revise it—she was working on *Persuasion* by then and was not feeling well. (Her final illness began in early 1816.) So she changed the main character's name to Catherine and likely did little else—as indicated by her advertisement to the reader suggesting that the novel might seem dated. Had she revised it much, she could have removed any dated elements. Austen did nothing more with the novel before she died a year later. Thus we have in *Northanger Abbey* an intriguing glimpse of Austen as a younger writer. This is fairly obvious while reading it. If you read *Persuasion* immediately afterward, you'll see the difference in writing style, sophistication, and mood.

ADVERTISEMENT,

BY THE AUTHORESS,

TO

NORTHANGER ABBEY.

This little work was finished in the year 1803, and intended for immediate publication. It was disposed of to a bookseller, it was even advertised, and why the business proceeded no farther, the author has never been able to learn. That any bookseller should think it worth while to purchase what he did not think it worth while to publish seems extraordinary.

As Austen's nephew James Edward Austen-Leigh tells us, once Henry Austen had control of the book again, he made sure to tell Crosby the publisher that the same anonymous author who had written *Pride and Prejudice*, which made some tidy profits for its publisher and made the author relatively famous, had written *Susan/Northanger Abbey*.

The social milieu of Bath

As in *Mansfield Park*, Northanger Abbey is one of the main settings of the book. We get to the Abbey via Bath. Our seventeen-year-old heroine Catherine Morland goes to Bath with her family's friends the Allens. They have a comfortable income, and can offer Catherine some of the pleasures that her own clergyman father can't afford for all ten of his children. Catherine meets Isabella Thorpe in Bath, along with her vain brother John Thorpe; she also meets the clever, mocking Henry Tilney and his sister Eleanor, whom she later visits at their home, Northanger Abbey. Catherine is sincere, good-natured, and unassuming, and aside from her fixation on melodramatic Gothic novels, she has a fairly keen mind. Henry Tilney immediately sees that Catherine has a fresh and frank nature, and he is drawn to her. She attracts John Thorpe as well, but more because she seems easy to impress. Catherine sees John's dullness and vanity quickly, but tolerates him for his sister's sake. Still, Catherine is far too good for Isabella, who reveals herself as an insincere, superficial flirt on the prowl for a rich husband. The inexperienced Catherine doesn't see this right away. She's too excited about going to balls and trading chilling horror novels with her new friend to look more closely at who she is.

The Orange Grove and Abbey Church by John Claude Nattes, from the print series *Bath Illustrated by a Series of Views*, 1806.

Milsom Street, by John Claude Nattes, from the book *Bath Illustrated by a Series of Views*, published in 1806.
This vantage provides a view of the town hall, market, and Abbey Church.

> *The novel has two lessons for its naïve heroine to learn: one, choose your friends wisely; and two, don't allow your imagination (or trashy popular culture) to run away with you.*

False friendship

Catherine learns one of her lessons in Bath, where the first friend she makes, Isabella Thorpe, turns out to be frivolous and untrustworthy. Isabella uses Catherine as a means to become closer to Catherine's brother James, who soon joins them in Bath. She also just wants a friend to parade about and whisper importantly with. Isabella and James eventually become engaged, but she dismisses him and flirts shamelessly when she believes she has found a richer man—Henry's older brother Captain Tilney.

Selfish flirt that she is, Isabella does demonstrate women's lack of control over their lives in Austen's time. Her widowed mother has little money, so Isabella goes to work looking for a good match in the husband-hunting oasis called Bath. She has little choice but to do this—her only hope for security lies in marrying well. When Isabella accepts James Morland's proposal, she hopes for a grand income—but alas, James will receive a mere four hundred pounds when they marry. Although he'll eventually inherit the Morland estate as well, which will draw in another four hundred pounds a year, Isabella is not satisfied with this more than adequate income. Thus she puts her fiancé on a back shelf and turns to the rake Captain Tilney, a richer man, leaving James and Catherine bewildered and hurt. Captain Tilney jilts her, though, and she gets just what she deserves.

Isabella is a product of a system that encourages women to think of money and a husband as the ultimate goals and beauty as a tool to achieve them. But Austen expects her readers to act honorably in the husband hunt, so she thwarts Isabella for showing no better impulse than to jilt a good man. Isabella exposes her falseness in a smarmy letter to Catherine, in which she hopes that Catherine will help her reconcile with James after Captain Tilney has dumped her: "Your kind offices will set all right" Isabella writes, "he is the only man I ever did or could love, and I trust you will convince him of it." But by the time Catherine receives this letter, she has learned her first lesson; she has the good sense to see through Isabella's pretense.

An undesirable suitor

Isabella's brother John Thorpe also makes a lousy companion; he's a loud-mouthed braggart who talks

ENVELOPE CONTENTS

- *A handwritten letter* from Jane Austen to her young niece, Cassandra Esten Austen, showing her sense of humor with the puzzle of "mirror writing." Written at Chawton in January 1817.

- *Jane dashed off* this handwritten poem for her brother Frank on the birth of his son. Written at Chawton and dated July 26, 1809.

This particular scene resembles something out of one of Catherine's Gothic novels: Isabella grabs one of Catherine's hands, Thorpe the other, and they and James try to make Catherine do as they command.

Mr John Thorpe

John Thorpe, Catherine's arrogant young suitor. Illustration by C. E. Brock from an early edition of *Northanger Abbey*, 1895.

of nothing but horses and his grand feats of driving and hunting. Once again, Austen shows us a timelessly irritating character. Thorpe is a liar as well as a bore: he lies to Catherine to convince her to abandon an outing with Henry and Eleanor Tilney. But she discovers his duplicity, so she is ready when he tries to manipulate her again in a similar fashion. When he lies to the Tilneys themselves about Catherine's plans for the afternoon in order to keep her to himself, Catherine must stand up to the Thorpes and do what is right, whatever the discomfort. This particular scene resembles something out of one of Catherine's Gothic novels: Isabella grabs one of Catherine's hands, Thorpe the other, and they and James try to make Catherine do as they command (they want her to go on an unchaperoned carriage ride to Clifton). But Catherine stands firm and insists on keeping her plans with the Tilneys, saying:

> "'Let me go, Mr. Thorpe; Isabella, do not hold me. . . . I will go after them,' said Catherine; 'wherever they are I will go after them. It does not signify talking. If I could not be persuaded into doing what I thought wrong, I never will be tricked into it.' And with these words she broke away and hurried off."

The Complicated Mr. Tilney

HENRY TILNEY IS A cryptic character. He appears far too sophisticated to be interested in a girl as naïve as Catherine Morland. He is glib and satirical, always ready to mock society's expectations and clichés. One wonders why he is so sardonic at so young an age. Consider what he says to Catherine at Northanger Abbey when he finds her near his mother's bedroom. Having discovered that she thought his father capable of killing his mother, he deflates her overactive imagination:

> "Does our education prepare us for such atrocities? Do our laws connive at them? Could they be perpetrated without being known, in a country like this, where social and literary intercourse is on such a footing; *where every man is surrounded by a neighborhood of voluntary spies,* and where roads and newspapers lay every thing open? Dearest Miss Morland, what ideas have you been admitting?" [italics added]

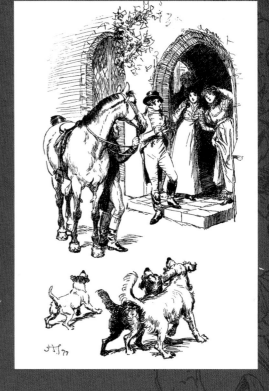

Consider the italicized bit of the quotation. Up until then, Henry is giving a pretty convincing lecture. But "neighborhood of voluntary spies"? With that attack, he undermines all that he is saying and even his culture itself. D. W. Harding noted this in 1940. So what is Austen doing here? Was she in a bad mood as she wrote it? Or did she mean to mock her culture? *Northanger Abbey* reads as a lighthearted novel, but Henry Tilney doesn't seem to fit, in part because he doesn't come across as light-hearted. He's a three-dimensional character, but he is hard to pin down.

Illustration of Henry Tilney by Hugh Thompson, from an early edition of *Northanger Abbey*.

Exploring the Gothic Genre

THE GOTHIC STYLE WAS everywhere in the eighteenth and nineteenth centuries—and given the popularity of books like Bram Stoker's 1897 novel *Dracula* and Anne Rice's modern vampire series, one could argue that the Gothic horror tradition never died (no pun intended). The Gothic novel first became popular with Horace Walpole's *The Castle of Otranto*, an English bestseller of 1764, or such is the general belief; in it, many supernatural events occur, all of them terrifying, all of them in a land far distant from England. As the eighteenth century continued, many writers copied Walpole's general plot: horrible but titillating things happen in a distant, usually Catholic enclave where the protagonists are far from "civilization." The strand of anti-Catholicism is unmistakable in the Gothic, as is its determination to shock and entertain readers in safe and stable Britain.

Most of the Gothic writers were not recording a story from far, far away—they were just English writers who had found their market. Many women of Austen's era read Gothic novels because they were easy to read (remember, in the eighteenth century women had no formal education) and real page-turners. Just as Gothic novels didn't require much education to read, they didn't require much education to write, either, and thus a number of women authors began writing them. Eliza Parsons, the English author of two of the "horrid" novels on Isabella's list, was a widow with eight children; writing Gothic novels helped her feed and clothe her family. Regina Maria Roche and Eleanor Sleath were two other women writers from the British Isles who were able to write the Gothic novel profitably—their books also appear on Isabella's list of novels. (All of those novels with the improbable titles that Austen mentions do exist, and you can find them at a library or bookstore near you, though you might have to special order them.)

Austen also profited indirectly from the Gothic, as it gave her a genre to write against. But however much Austen mocked the Gothic, she also understood it—she knew English author Ann Radcliffe's work well enough to "recommend" and laugh at it in two books. In *Emma*, Harriet recommends that Robert Martin read Radcliffe's 1791 novel *The Romance of the Forest*, and of course in *Northanger Abbey* Radcliffe's *The Mysteries of Udolpho* brings the Tilneys and Catherine into a full understanding of each other. *The Italian* (1797), which Isabella and Catherine plan to read together, is also by Radcliffe. Austen presumably read Matthew Gregory Lewis's

Here Austen subtly presents a more realistic version of the drama in a Gothic novel: a young woman will not likely find herself forced by nefarious forces to wed an ogre in a distant land, but a young woman may well be manipulated by friends and family into doing something unacceptable.

A "nice" young man

The young man Catherine runs to after physically freeing herself from the Thorpes stands in opposition to almost everything about John Thorpe. Henry Tilney has a perceptive mind and the gift of quick-moving, intelligent conversation that might actually be worth listening to. He clearly appreciates Catherine's straightforward, unaffected nature, even as he pokes fun at her occasional silliness. Though he himself reads Gothic novels, he sees their excess and will pontificate against careless language everywhere, including in women's letters and conversations. While walking with Catherine and his sister one day, he makes fun of Catherine for calling Ann Radcliffe's *The Mysteries of Udolpho* (which they've both read) the "nicest book in the world." She responds by saying, "'. . . but it *is* a nice book, and why should I not call it so?'" Henry responds like someone who has recently memorized key passages in the *Oxford English Dictionary*:

"Very true," said Henry, "and this is a very nice day, and we are taking a very nice walk, and you are two very nice young ladies. Oh! it is a very nice word indeed!—it does for every thing. Originally perhaps it was applied only to express neatness, propriety, delicacy, or refinement;—people were nice in their dress, in their sentiments, or their choice. But now every commendation on every subject is comprised in that one word."

Henry enjoys mocking the mundane and commonplace. His comments are fascinating and new to Catherine, who can never tell whether he's serious or not, or even exactly what he's getting at. Clearly she will benefit from association with this intelligent and thought-provoking young man, but Catherine herself doesn't think of whether she'll benefit from Henry or not—she falls in love with him because he's handsome and kind.

The lessons are clear here: a wise young woman chooses her friends carefully and can't be fooled by shallow protestations of affection and devotion; it is actions that matter, not just words. They are simple lessons but people still need to learn them. The timelessness of Austen again reveals itself.

Satirizing Gothic novels

Jane Austen did fear that her second lesson, not to let oneself be carried away by the horrific plots

popular Gothic novel *The Monk*, a creepy and overtly anti-Catholic tale that takes place in Spain; she mentions this novel in *Northanger Abbey* as well. So Austen might have satirized Gothic novels, but she also read them. Purely for research purposes, of course.

In *Northanger Abbey*, Austen follows Radcliffe's general approach to the Gothic: Radcliffe usually presents scary and supernatural events in her novels, but then she explains them all in the end as coincidences or schemes perpetrated by a nefarious count or some such villain. At least one other writer copied Radcliffe—Francis Lathom, writer of *The Midnight Bell*, which is also on Isabella's list—scared his readers with impossible, terrifying events, and then explained them. So when Austen implies in *Northanger Abbey* that something is mysteriously wrong at the Abbey, and then shows that Catherine is all wrong about it, she was doing what other writers had done. The satire of the Gothic, though, was pretty original.

For more information on the Gothic and to get started with your own "horrid" reading, see Devendra Varma's writing on anything Gothic. Or you can just pick up Ann Radcliffe's *The Mysteries of Udolpho*, which is still good reading after more than two hundred years.

The graveyard of Saint Mary's Church in Whitby, which inspired Bram Stoker to set part of his classic Gothic novel *Dracula* in the English town. Photograph circa 1995.

ONLY ONE PUBLICATION, the *British Critic*, reviewed *Northanger Abbey* and *Persuasion* when the novels first appeared after Austen's death. An anonymous reviewer expresses his "most unfeigned regret" over the fact that these two novels will be the last that readers will be able to read by Jane Austen, whose novels "display a degree of excellence that has not been often surpassed."

This same reviewer goes on to offer a few criticisms in a generally good review:

> *Northanger Abbey* is one of the very best of Miss Austen's productions, and will every way repay the time and trouble of perusing it. Some of the incidents in it are rather improbable, and the character of General Tilney seems to have been drawn from imagination, for it is not a very probable character, and is not pourtrayed [sic] with our authoress's usual taste and judgment. There is also a considerable want of delicacy in all the circumstances of Catherine's visit to the Abbey . . .

The review is telling—one can see here what Austen was up against as a writer. Though the reviewer does not specify what wants "delicacy" about the scenes at the Abbey, one imagines the reviewer is referring to the relative freedom Henry Tilney and Catherine have together while at the Abbey. For instance, when Henry catches her in the vicinity of his mother's former bedroom, they are alone together in a large gallery. The three young people—Henry, his sister Eleanor, and Catherine—also have the house to themselves for a few days while the General is away.

Henry's ability to read Catherine may also seem a bit intimate; a good girl, perhaps, would not be so transparent to her suitor. The review conveys how lightly Austen had to tiptoe while writing. It must have been very easy to write an indelicate passage in 1817.

of Gothic novels, would not seem so timeless. When Austen regained control of her novel in 1816, the Gothic novel was a bit less popular than it had been in 1803 when she first sold the novel: one of the key targets for her sharp pen wasn't the target it had previously been. So in the advertisement that Austen attached to the beginning of the novel, in which she tells the reader that the first publisher who bought the novel chose not to publish it, she alerts readers that her writing might appear dated.

> *As it turns out, warnings about becoming too engrossed in a horror story can never be dated, for the teenager's desire to be safely frightened is still very much alive.*

The various horror movies today that involve chainsaws and pretty women are proof that young people still find chilling images entertaining. So Austen's lesson to Catherine still has force in the twenty-first century.

When Austen wrote the first draft of *Susan/Northanger Abbey*, Gothic novels were all the rage. These books were usually set in southern or eastern Europe, in some dark and isolated locale, with plots that involved intrigue, murder, kidnapping, and the supernatural. The vulnerable but virtuous Gothic heroine usually found herself in some grave danger, and some writers

Catherine prepares to read a Gothic novel. Engraving by R. Graves after a painting by R. W. Bass, 1892.

Young Orphan in the Cemetery by Eugene Delacroix, 1824. The painting's title and the emotion on the girl's face contain echoes of the type of novel Catherine and Isabella like to read.

incorporated rape and incest to make the books all the more juicy.

This over-the-top style fairly begged for satire; the attentive reader can see that Austen is making fun of the Gothic novel from page one. Look at the way the novel opens:

> No one who had ever seen Catherine Morland in her infancy, would have supposed her born to be an heroine. Her situation in life, the character of her father and mother, her own person and disposition, were all equally against her. Her father was a clergyman, without being neglected, or poor, and a very respectable man, though his name was Richard—and he had never been handsome. He had a considerable independence, besides two good livings—and he was not in the least addicted to locking up his daughters. Her mother was a woman of useful plain sense, with a good temper, and, what is more remarkable, with a good constitution.

The Gothic heroine was often an orphan, or her family didn't have much money, or her surviving parent was desperately ill—and yes, a father or a cruel guardian could possibly lock the heroine in an inescapable bedroom.

The frivolous Isabella Thorpe also reads many Gothic novels and encourages Catherine in reading them; she has put together a list of novels for Catherine's book list:

> "'I will read you their names directly; here they are, in my pocket-book. Castle of Wolfenbach, Clermont, Mysterious Warnings, Necromancer of the Black Forest, Midnight Bell, Orphan of the Rhine, *and* Horrid Mysteries. *Those will last us some time.*'"

Catherine is intrigued, but she wants to make sure she is reading the right stuff: "'Yes . . . but are they all horrid, are you sure they are all horrid?'" Catherine's insistence on being scared is amusing, and again shows Jane Austen's deft writing—the mixture of humor and lessons works well.

Imagination run wild

While Catherine slowly figures out that Isabella is not such a good friend after all, she befriends Henry Tilney's younger sister Eleanor and receives an invitation to visit the family at Northanger Abbey when they leave Bath. Gothic novels were often set in an ancient castle, or the ruins of an old church, or even, say, an abbey—so naturally, Catherine is wild to explore Northanger Abbey's cobwebbed corridors. Knowing well how the Gothic novel typically unfolds, Austen portrays the Tilney home as quite the opposite of the typical menacing castle. The Abbey is an open, airy place fitted up in the modern style, with no locked doors or hidden secrets. There, General Tilney, the father of the family,

With Henry's help, Catherine must rationally face the fact that she has read a few too many Gothic novels.

treats Catherine especially hospitably—but she does not trust him. She convinces herself that General Tilney has something to hide, and becomes suspicious that he has killed his wife, the beloved mother of Eleanor and Henry who died suddenly of an illness some years before. Henry catches her in this folly and helps her put the brakes on her fanciful imagination. With Henry's help, Catherine must rationally face the fact that she has read a few too many Gothic novels, that she is not staying in a haunted abbey with a murderer as host, and that she really needs to grow up.

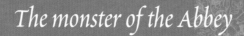

The monster of the Abbey

But as it turns out, Catherine is not entirely wrong about General Tilney: he is not a murderer, but he's not a nice guy, either. His generous hospitality, it turns out, stems from his belief that children, he was able to represent the whole family to the General in the most respectable light." But Thorpe isn't finished: he hints that Catherine will also likely inherit a tidy package from the childless but rich Mr. Allen. General Tilney, a greedy and selfish man, believes this without question, and determines that his son Henry should marry this woman who is apparently worth "ten or fifteen thousand pounds" at least.

Catherine's loving parents may well want to see if Henry loses interest in a young woman whose family income cannot match his.

The real "horror" story here is the General's mercenary tyranny: when he finds that Catherine does not have anywhere near what he thought, only a few hundred pounds, he furiously has her removed from his house.

Catherine belongs to a rich family. He swallows John Thorpe's tale of her, which Thorpe tells because he intends to marry Catherine himself. In a conversation with the General early in the novel, Thorpe tries to puff up his own image by improving Catherine's, so he greatly exaggerates her wealth: "by doubling what he chose to think the amount of Mr. Morland's preferment, trebling his private fortune, bestowing a rich aunt, and sinking half the

Never mind that the General has approved of her so far. Her personality does not matter: only her father's income does. He sends her home by public carriage, a second-class way to travel. We readers naturally dislike the General for being so cruel to his daughter's good-hearted friend, especially today, when (we flatter ourselves) money is less important in marriage.

The 1986 BBC film *Northanger Abbey* adds more reasons to despise General Tilney: he is also an inveterate gambler who is bankrupting the family. This little touch helps modern viewers understand why the General should be so upset that Catherine is not rich. Austen readers know that for an arrogant rich man of Austen's era, a woman's not having a fortune was enough for a father to reject her as a possible match for his son. But today many viewers need additional convincing as to why a man would suddenly throw his daughter's friend out of his house.

A *hero comes to the rescue*

Luckily, Henry Tilney loves Catherine enough to ignore the relatively small financial package that is actually attached to her and comes after her to propose. They can't marry immediately, though: Mr. and Mrs. Morland understand that Catherine's engagement to Henry is "a match beyond the claims of their daughter," which is perhaps why they require that their seventeen-year-old daughter and her twenty-five-year-old suitor wait before marrying until the General agrees to give his permission. The loving parents may well want to see if Henry loses interest in a young woman whose family income cannot match his. But Henry is one of the good guys—he stays true to Catherine and they eventually marry. Once again, money can't get in the way of true love.

Portrait thought to be of a young Jane Austen by British painter Ozias Humphry, circa 1788-1789. Jane would have been about fourteen.

Chapter Six

PERSUASION

"When any two young people take it into their heads to marry, they are pretty sure by perseverance to carry their point, be they ever so poor, or ever so imprudent, or ever so little likely to be necessary to each other's ultimate comfort."

Jane Austen gives us her most mature work

and her last complete one in *Persuasion*. Written in 1815-1816 by a forty-year-old woman whose health was deteriorating as she finished the novel and who must have been assessing her life from middle age, the book tells of regret, of longing, of second chances and reunion. It suggests a possibility of rebirth, of recovering from hard times and emerging into a better future. Austen's oldest heroine, the twenty-seven-year-old Anne Elliot, escapes her mean-spirited family to live a life that intrigued Austen herself, a life at sea, which Austen heard about frequently from her two seafaring brothers.

> *Persuasion provides a strong ending to her writing career and an escape that satisfies, an escape we'd wish for Jane Austen herself.*

Persuasion's heroine, Anne Elliot, is not introduced in the first paragraph of the novel, despite being the main character. She is merely referred to as the book opens and not mentioned again until the end of paragraph seven, and there we learn this of her: "she was only Anne." This dismissive sentence

The Convalescent by Jules Emile Saintin, circa mid-1800s.

A Glimpse of the British Class System

THE TRUTH IS, FROM THE tippy-top of the British social system, Anne's father Sir Walter isn't much; his cousin the viscountess would likely smile condescendingly if she knew that he likes to gaze at his name in the Baronetage. The titled hierarchy of Britain is a complicated system, but it's fascinating and Sir Walter (along with many others) cares about it very much. Jane Austen cared about it a lot less than Sir Walter does, but it's worthwhile to understand the system she was laughing at in *Persuasion*, so let's take a quick look at the British class system.

At the top of the ladder sits royalty. This group includes the king or queen—"the sovereign"—and beneath him or her sit the Prince of Wales and other males of the royal family. Royal daughters and granddaughters and mothers and aunts also belong to the royal class, but during Austen's time they would have had less importance than men (and then Victoria came along…). Beneath royalty sits the nobility, or the "peerage." These are all titled positions originally awarded by a sovereign. From top to bottom, they rank this way: duke and duchess, marquess and marchioness, earl and countess, viscount and viscountess,

baron and baroness. Each of these positions is hereditary; that is, the first-born son typically would inherit the title.

Next comes the gentry. At the top of this class sit the baronets, followed by the knights. Sir Walter is a baronet, which is why his name appears in the Baronetage. Sir William Lucas of *Pride and Prejudice* is a knight. Note that both are called "sir;" this fact likely makes Sir Walter grind his teeth while sleeping. But Sir William's position as a knight is merely a lifetime rank, and his sons will not be called "Sir." Sir Walter's title is hereditary, but for all his rank and privilege and vanity, he could not hold a seat in the House of Lords, for anyone who is not a member of the peerage is a commoner. (One imagines that Sir Walter hates that word.)

To clarify, anyone not a member of the peerage—which would include the vast majority of British citizens and all of the ladies and gentlemen of the gentry—is a commoner. So knights, in spite of visions of Arthur sitting at a round table, aren't all that lofty a class after all, and baronets are just a cut above knights. So don't let Sir Walter's pompous behavior mislead you—he's no nobleman.

demonstrates her place in her family's hierarchy. Sir Walter Elliot appears first in the novel, the vain and self-involved father of three daughters, a widower who lost his perceptive and capable wife when his daughters were teenagers. As a father and role model Sir Walter is not promising: his favorite book is the Baronetage, an extended family tree of all the baronets in England, and his favorite page is the one that bears his own name, "Elliot of Kellynch-Hall." His vanity also shows in the number of mirrors in the house. As Austen wryly puts it, "Few women could think more of their personal appearance than he did, nor could the valet of any new made lord be more delighted with the place he held in society."

> *Sir Walter is a fop and a fool. But he's also the most powerful man in this corner of Somersetshire.*

Anne's sisters are not promising characters, either. Like her father, the eldest daughter Elizabeth thinks of herself as a very important person, for she became the lady of a baronet's house at age sixteen when her mother died. Austen describes Elizabeth as "repulsive and unsisterly"—quite an insult, given Jane Austen's close relationship with her sister Cassandra. At twenty-nine, Elizabeth is still good-looking, but is nearing the "years of danger" for she is still not married. She loathes seeing the Baronetage; listing merely her name and birth date, it is a constant reminder of her failure to make a good match.

The youngest Elliot daughter, Mary, has married into the second family in the area, behind only the Elliots themselves, the Musgroves of Uppercross. While not quite as vain as Elizabeth, Mary shows her self-centeredness through her hypochondria and constant reminders that she comes from a better family than her in-laws.

The other daughter

One would expect Sir Walter to have children like Elizabeth and Mary, but Anne has the unexpected nature: patient, intelligent, capable, and kind. We learn that she is much like her mother, a "sensible, and amiable" woman whose only mistake in life was to become infatuated with Sir Walter's good looks and title. Without her, Anne finds herself at the mercy of her father and sisters, who have no regard for her: "Anne, with an elegance of mind and sweetness of character, which must have placed her high with any people of real understanding, was nobody with either father or sister."

Anne is a persevering soul, though, who makes the best of things, so she tolerates her family. Her emotional sustenance comes from her relationship

with a family friend, Lady Russell, who was her mother's good friend and still lives nearby at Kellynch Lodge. But Lady Russell is easily impressed by rank and property, which has its consequences for Anne.

> "*Anne, with an elegance of mind and sweetness of character, which must have placed her high with any people of real understanding, was nobody with either father or sister.*"

Anne's mistake

Surrounded by rank-conscious people, Anne allowed their practical concerns to direct her life eight years before the novel opens, in 1806. She fell in love then with a young commander in the navy, Captain Wentworth: while visiting his brother in the neighborhood where the Elliots live, he proposed to the nineteen-year-old Anne, and she accepted. But Sir Walter, Elizabeth, and Lady Russell worked together to persuade Anne to retract her acceptance, for Captain

This 1802 engraving, *Lordly Elevation* by James Gillray, suggests
the preening vanity of Sir Walter Elliot.

Wentworth had no fortune. Lady Russell particularly
argued against the match, thinking of it this way:

> *"Anne Elliot, with all her claims of birth,
> beauty, and mind, to throw herself away
> at nineteen; involve herself at nineteen in
> an engagement with a young man, who had
> nothing but himself to recommend him,
> and no hopes of attaining affluence, but in
> the chances of a most uncertain profession,
> and no connexions to secure even his
> farther rise in that profession; would be,
> indeed, a throwing away, which she grieved
> to think of!"*

In Austen's time, love was not enough to justify
a marriage on its own; in the eyes of the high-born
gentry, Wentworth is a loser. Anne is young and
impressionable in 1806; she acquiesces to Lady Russell
and her family. Anne persuades herself that she's
actually doing Wentworth a favor in not marrying him;
because Sir Walter disapproved of the match, he would
not give Wentworth a dowry along with Anne's hand.

Anne cannot forget Wentworth, though; after he
leaves the neighborhood, she sinks into a depression
that swallows her pretty youth and lasts until the
novel commences, in 1814, when Wentworth comes

back into the area. Much has changed over the eight years he has been gone. Because of Sir Walter's lavish spending habits, the Elliots have been forced to move to Bath, where one may live luxuriously at less cost than in a country estate. (Austen knew first-hand how this worked, since her family had done much the same thing when she was twenty-five.) Sir Walter and Elizabeth have gone ahead to Bath to find a suitable house, while Anne stays with Mary at Uppercross. Sir Walter has rented out Kellynch-Hall to Admiral and Mrs. Croft, coincidentally Captain Wentworth's brother-in-law and sister. The Crofts do not know that Wentworth was once engaged to Anne Elliot, and Elizabeth and Sir Walter have all but forgotten that little wrinkle in the life of "only Anne."

Captain Wentworth comes back into Somersetshire to visit his sister, and he returns as a rich and confident man, having accumulated considerable wealth as the captain of several ships. Through hard work and perseverance, Wentworth has succeeded in life. He has not married, but he is still angry with Anne Elliot for rejecting him. So their reunion in Somersetshire is not a happy one: both publicly pretend their romance never happened while quietly dealing with the teeming emotions evoked by seeing each other again.

Persuasion shows all the characteristics of another Cinderella story, down to the two mean stepsisters, but in this story, it seems that Prince Charming has come and gone already. Because this is Jane Austen, however, we know not to give up on Anne.

A view of the sea

In this novel, her last, Jane Austen does several things she has not done before—the most obvious new aspect is the larger canvas of the novel. She goes beyond the country house and single parish in *Persuasion*—she gives us the seashore and the high seas. She presents to readers the British navy and the war with France (though she gives no specifics). She offers a glimpse of seafaring—as a means to wealth and as an appealing draw to the adventurous and resourceful mind.

The ocean also presents a place of escape for Austen and her heroine. While Anne is staying with her sister Mary and the Musgroves at Uppercross, the young people go on a trip to the seaside town of Lyme. Austen describes their first sight of the ocean with real feeling:

> *"The party from Uppercross passing down . . . soon found themselves on the sea shore, and lingering only, as all must linger and gaze on a first return to the sea, who ever deserve to look on it at all."*

The group from Uppercross consists of Anne, Mary, Mary's husband, his pretty younger sisters Henrietta

ENVELOPE CONTENTS

- *A handwritten page* from chapter 11 of the original manuscript of *Persuasion* by Jane Austen, showing her edits. This novel is the only one for which evidence of her editing decisions survives.

- *A letter from* Jane Austen to her seafaring brother Frank, written after the death of their father and dated January 20, 1805.

Making One's Fortune in the Navy

THE SEA IS A PLACE OF possibility, where a man "who had nothing but himself to recommend him" can improve his position in life through committed work. The hopeless snob Sir Walter objects to the navy as "the means of bringing persons of obscure birth into undue distinction, and raising men to honours which their fathers and grandfathers never dreamt of."

Sir Walter had reason to be concerned. The British navy was unlike the British army in that a man did not have to buy a commission to become an officer. Poor boys or relatively penniless younger sons from gentry families could rise up on their own merit. This isn't to say that advancement in the navy was easy; in the British socio-economic system, moving out of one's class into a higher one required real mettle. But Austen knew the possibilities of the navy firsthand: her brothers Francis and Charles, both younger sons from a financially struggling family, enlisted in the Royal Navy.

Francis "Frank" Austen became a vice admiral and was knighted. Charles Austen, despite being shipwrecked, eventually became a rear admiral. This would put both brothers at the same rank as *Persuasion*'s Admiral Croft, and higher than Captain Wentworth.

and Louisa, and Captain Wentworth, who has been flirting with Louisa. While the party walks along the shoreline one day, impulsive Louisa jumps down a steep wall into Wentworth's arms. She becomes over-exuberant and Wentworth can't catch her when she jumps again; she hits the ground hard enough to knock her senseless. While everyone else panics, Anne keeps her cool and directs matters, sending for a doctor and getting Louisa safely to a bed in a nearby house.

The accident jars Wentworth out of his rigid resolve not to favor Anne Elliot. As Louisa lies motionless, Anne proves that she remains the same fine and able person Wentworth loved eight years before, and he cannot pretend to ignore her any longer. It will take more than this to bring them together—they go their separate ways after the Lyme trip. Later, the two lovers find each other in Bath and become engaged. As the novel ends, Anne's truest happiness comes via the sea: we learn that Anne "gloried in being a sailor's wife." This is perhaps Austen's strongest statement of a heroine's happiness as one of her novels ends.

Jane Austen's seaside tryst

Jane Austen adored the sea. She had reason to—her beloved older brother Frank was a sailor who ascended the officer ranks in the English navy. She took great interest in his career, as she did in

her younger brother Charles, who was also a naval officer. And Jane Austen had good memories of seaside resorts. Her family took at least one outing to Lyme in 1803, and she had her own private romantic reason for portraying the shore positively—perhaps her most meaningful love affair. We have only a snippet of Cassandra's memory to go on, told to her niece Caroline Austen, who in turn reported it to Austen's great-nephew William Austen-Leigh and her great-great-nephew Richard Arthur Austen-Leigh. Caroline tells us that while Cassandra and Jane were visiting "some seaside place," a gentleman there "seemed greatly attracted by my Aunt Jane—I suppose it was an intercourse of some weeks—and that when they had to part (I imagine he was a visitor also, but his family might have lived near) he was urgent to know where they would be the next summer, implying or perhaps saying that he should be there also, wherever it might be. I can only say that the impression left on Aunt Cassandra was that he had fallen in love with her sister, and was quite in earnest. Soon afterwards they heard of his death."

James Edward Austen-Leigh also writes of this lost seaside romance, which he also heard from Cassandra; he believes that if Jane Austen loved anyone, she loved this man. Little is known of this mysterious romance, but it's likely that Austen was in Devon when the romance took place; Austen biographer Park Honan believes she was at Sidmouth, a fashionable resort town in the early nineteenth century. If this is the case, the

The Naval Dockyard at Deptford by Samuel Scott, circa mid-1700s.

View of a Country House, oil painting by an anonymous member of the British School, circa 1840.

romance would have taken place in 1801, when Austen was twenty-five.

Whether this unnamed man was the love of her life or not, Austen clearly had fine associations with the sea. As she wrote her last complete manuscript, she could well have been remembering her own youth, walking on the arm of a young suitor who could hardly wait to see her again. If so, it's not surprising that Captain Frederick Wentworth notices Anne Elliot again at the shore, where he's drawn by "her very regular, very pretty features, having the bloom and freshness of youth restored by the fine wind which had been blowing on her complexion, and by the animation of eye which it had also produced." There on the coast two other men also pay unexpected attention to Anne: she attracts her cousin Mr. Elliot, who has just arrived from Sidmouth, and she even draws the heartbroken Captain Benwick out of his shell by talking to him about poetry with intelligence and sympathy.

The author widens her focus

Before writing *Persuasion*, Jane Austen had written with a tight focus on country families, observing and recording often overlooked details of the personalities and society that surrounded her, and the results were astounding, far beyond her expectations. But she is ready, in *Persuasion*, to reach out further and widen her focus. Austen was clearly thinking about her art in the last year of her life. In December 1816, after finishing *Persuasion*, she wrote a letter to her teenage nephew James Edward, the same James Edward Austen-Leigh who would

> " *I can only say that the impression left on Aunt Cassandra was that he had fallen in love with her sister, and was quite in earnest. Soon afterwards they heard of his death.* "

eventually write *Memoir of Jane Austen*, from which we draw so much information about his famous aunt. James Edward at the time was writing novels himself, and apparently several pages were missing from one of his manuscripts. Austen jokes that it's a good thing that she wasn't visiting him at the time of the "theft," as she would have been accused of stealing his good ideas. To this she adds this commentary on her art:

Lyme Regis, from Charmouth, Dorset, an engraving of the seashore by William Daniell, circa 1817-1825.

"*I do not think however that any theft of that sort would be really very useful to me. What should I do with your strong, manly, spirited Sketches, full of Variety & Glow?— How could I possibly join them on to the little bit (two Inches wide) of Ivory on which I work with so fine a Brush, as produces little effect after much labour?*"

By the end of 1816, after several of her books had sold out, after all the good reviews of her work, and after she learned that the Prince Regent admired her novels and invited her to dedicate a book to him, Austen knew that her work produced far more than "little effect." Her comment is modest and perhaps ironic. But it also suggests that she's thinking about the scope of her work. She knows she does not write worldly books, that her works consist of amusing and interior pieces, highly personal and yet communal as well—involving a community of family and neighbors and generations, living and aspiring together, for better and for worse. Given the artistic self-awareness expressed here, Austen seems to recognize that she had begun to broaden her scope beyond that bit of ivory—she has already done this in *Persuasion*. We can only wonder what further widening of her vision Austen intended to pursue as she wrote those words.

An inner voice emerges

There is another added dimension in *Persuasion*: as the novel unfolds, Austen gives us more direct descriptions of what is going on in her heroine's mind. For instance, when Anne first sees Wentworth again, she is flustered, but glad to have the meeting behind her: "'It is over! it is over!' she repeated to herself again, and again, in nervous gratitude. 'The worst is over!'" Immediately after thinking this, Anne tries to tell herself that much has changed, that her feelings have ebbed for Wentworth. But she can't fool herself: "Alas! With all her reasonings, she found, that to retentive feelings eight years may be little more than nothing."

We also see a grim humor in Anne's thoughts. As the young people walk together on an autumn day, Anne listens to Louisa declare to Wentworth that she would stand by her man whatever the cost; Anne is acutely aware that she did not stand by Wentworth eight years earlier. Wentworth responds by exclaiming, "'I honour you!'" Before hearing this, Anne had been trying to think of lines of poetry that would help her enjoy the day. In response to Wentworth's admiration of Louisa, her thoughts of poetry turn against her: "Anne could not immediately fall into a quotation again. The sweet scenes of autumn were for a while put by—unless some tender sonnet, fraught with the apt analogy of the declining year, with declining

happiness, and the images of youth and hope, and spring, all gone together, blessed her memory."

We primarily see Anne's emotions in the novel, but we also see more of a male protagonist's innermost thoughts than in other Austen novels. Austen tells us this of Captain Wentworth: "He had not forgiven Anne Elliot. She had used him ill;

> *We also see more of a male protagonist's innermost thoughts than in other Austen novels.*

deserted and disappointed him; and worse, she had shewn a feebleness of character in doing so, which his own decided, confident temper could not endure. She had given him up to oblige others. It had been the effect of over-persuasion. It had been weakness and timidity." We also learn that he is ready to marry: "He had a heart for either of the Miss Musgroves, if they could catch it; a heart, in short, for any pleasing young woman who came in his way, excepting Anne Elliot." Although Wentworth's feelings toward Anne seem stubbornly opposed to her, he does not fully know his own mind yet—which Austen wants to show us as well.

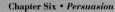

> *"Anne Elliot was not out of his thoughts, when he more seriously described the woman he should wish to meet with. 'A strong mind, with sweetness of manner,' made the first and the last of the description."*

A careful reader uncovers in Austen a writer unafraid of laughing at everything false and self-important.

Sharpening her narrative voice

Jane Austen as narrator speaks much more openly in *Persuasion* than in previous works, resulting in some blunt, even harsh, words. Consider the description of Dick Musgrove, Mary's brother-in-law who served under Captain Wentworth and died at sea. Mrs. Musgrove has become sentimental about her son, but Austen tells us of another side of the man:

He had, in fact, though his sisters were now doing all they could for him, by calling him "poor Richard," been nothing better than a thick-headed, unfeeling, unprofitable Dick Musgrove, who had never done any thing to entitle himself to more than the abbreviation of his name, living or dead.

Then Austen tells us this of Mrs. Musgrove's mourning over her son: ". . . Captain Wentworth should be allowed some credit for the self-command with which he attended to her large fat sighings over the destiny of a son, whom alive nobody had cared for." Austen doesn't hold back in exposing the true nature of the dead sailor or the hypocrisy of his mother.

Austen writes vindictively of Elizabeth, whom she leaves in her unmarried state as the novel closes. Elizabeth had high hopes of marrying her cousin and her father's heir, Mr. Elliot; when Mr. Elliot was friendly with Sir Walter and her in Bath, she expected Mr. Elliot to propose to her. But he doesn't. Austen says this of the disappointed Elizabeth: "It would be well for the eldest sister if she were equally satisfied with her situation [as Anne is after marrying Wentworth], for a change is not very probable there. She had soon the mortification of seeing Mr. Elliot withdraw; and no one of proper condition has since presented himself to raise even the unfounded hopes which sunk with him." Austen makes clear here that she intends to punish Elizabeth with at least a few more years of a Baronetcy that lists only her name and birth date.

An undeserved reputation

Those who think Austen is ever the gentle author might be surprised by such harsh comments from the sweet lady. This makes one think of E.M. Forster, who adores Austen, but notes that he himself reads her "with mouth open and the mind closed." He admits that when he takes up an Austen novel, he does not think critically. He describes Jane Austen as an idol, his idol, and "Like all regular churchgoers, he scarcely notices what is being said." So does Forster miss Austen's sharp comments like those above? Perhaps—and maybe this is why Austen is thought of as such a tame writer. Austen's brother Henry Austen also misrepresents his sister to some degree. Consider this description of dear Jane: "Though the frailties, foibles, and follies of others could not escape her immediate detection, yet even on their vices did she never trust herself to comment with unkindness." What? Did Henry read his sister's last novel? (There's also some sharp commentary from Mr. Henry Tilney in *Northanger Abbey*, the companion novel that was published with *Persuasion*.) Though Henry arranged to have Austen's last two novels published, perhaps he too scarcely noticed what he was reading. But a careful reader uncovers in Austen a writer unafraid of laughing at everything false and self-important. When these final novels were published after Austen's death,

Austen often turned a keen eye on her own society. This illustration from *Rudolph Ackermann's Repository of Arts*, published in 1822, depicts a woman in evening dress.

Chapter Six • *Persuasion*

in 1817, a reviewer for the *British Critic* praised Jane Austen and her realistic scenes: "Her merit consists altogether in her remarkable talent for observation; no ridiculous phrase, no affected sentiment, no foolish pretension seems to escape her notice. It is scarcely possible to read her novels, without meeting with some of one's own absurdities reflected back upon one's conscience . . ."

Austen's talent for keen observation isn't often questioned, but her critics sometimes complain about the confined range of her works and her modest goals.

Austen's talent for keen observation isn't often questioned, but her critics sometimes complain about the confined range of her works and her modest goals. Enter D.W. Harding and his famous essay on Austen, "Regulated Hatred: An Aspect of the Work of Jane Austen," in which he chronicles

his conversion into an Austen-lover. Harding describes Austen's reputation as "a delicate satirist, revealing with inimitable lightness of touch the comic foibles and amiable weaknesses of the people whom she lived amongst and liked." Harding had been led to believe that Austen is a gentle writer who writes of gentle topics—and this belief made him averse to reading Jane Austen. But he reads her anyway—a literary critic has to know his stuff—and he finds that "delicate" simply doesn't fit well. In Harding's view, Austen is instead a savvy writer whose "books are, as she meant them to be, read and enjoyed by precisely the sort of people whom she disliked; she is a literary classic of the society which attitudes like hers, held widely enough, would undermine." She knew she would never get away with publishing rants against the systems of inheritance that elevated unworthy snobs and fools while holding back intelligent, deserving people without great wealth.

Jane Austen tucked criticism of her society into romance, humor, and moral lessons, knowing that often the very same people she meant to mock would miss the jokes and jabs directed at them.

Love Token by William Powell Frith, circa 1800s.

Austen speaks for herself

Jane Austen doesn't step quite as carefully in *Persuasion*. While her other novels gathered many words of praise for the lessons embedded in them (learn to control your emotions, don't judge others too quickly,

In 1818, the general belief was that young people should marry only after consulting their family and friends and following their advice.

and the like) the same *British Critic* reviewer quoted above notes that Austen offers questionable advice in *Persuasion*, despite its good points:

> It is manifestly the work of the same mind, and contains parts of very great merit; among them, however, we certainly should not number its *moral*, which seems to be, that young people should always marry according to their own inclinations and upon their own judgment.

This statement sounds almost completely backward today, but this reviewer expresses the accepted perspective on marriage during Austen's life: in 1818, the general belief was that young people should marry only after consulting their family and friends and following their advice. The review inadvertently conveys the same attitudes that defeated Anne Elliot's attempt to resist her father and sister and friend when she accepted Wentworth's marriage proposal at age nineteen. In this review, Anne's strength in recognizing and taking her second chance at happiness despite her narrow-minded family's opinions is seen as misguided and a bad example. This reviewer expects a woman writer to be "delicate." Jane Austen did not always agree, thank fortune.

The question of money

Women in Austen's society learned to take advice and not to ask hard questions, which left them vulnerable—to heartbreak, as with Anne, or worse. The situation of Anne's friend Mrs. Smith, who also lives in Bath, is Austen's most extreme depiction of a helpless gentry woman fallen on hard times. Anne's former school chum married an extravagant man who died two years earlier, leaving her with a tangle of business affairs to deal with. So the widow Mrs. Smith is left poor, living in humble lodgings, "unable even to afford herself the comfort of a servant." On top of all this, she has rheumatism and cannot walk on her own. Anne's cousin and Mr. Smith's good friend Mr. Elliot has left Mrs. Smith all the more vulnerable. Mr. Smith trusted his friend enough to make him the executor of his estate. But upon Mr. Smith's death, Mr. Elliot does not do anything to settle his estate.

> *We learn that Mrs. Smith owns a property in the West Indies that could provide her with a decent income, but a woman does not have the legal authority to look into such matters and Mrs. Smith doesn't have the money to hire a lawyer.*

After he marries Anne, Captain Wentworth comes to Mrs. Smith's aid, "by writing for her, acting for her, and seeing her through all the petty difficulties of the case, with the activity and exertion of a fearless man . . ." Austen's phrase "fearless man" conveys her frustration that it takes a man to settle even "petty" issues—a woman cannot legally attend to such matters herself, even when they concern her own property.

Had Captain Wentworth not come to Mrs. Smith's aid, her situation could only have worsened with no income. Once her money ran out, she could sell all her property—any furniture or jewelry—to cover her

Louisa impulsively jumps from the wall at Lyme and is knocked senseless. Illustration by Hugh Thomson from an early edition of *Persuasion*, circa 1880.

A gentry woman caught in a situation like Mrs. Smith's might have to sell her belongings before acknowledging defeat and going out to work. *At the Pawnbroker's* by Thomas Reynolds Lamont, circa 1800s.

debts. When that money had run out, given that she couldn't even admit failure and sink to the level of the working class by getting a job—she can't walk, after all, so she can't work—she could have ended up in debtor's prison or worse.

Anne's situation is not exactly rosy, either, not without Captain Wentworth. Though her father Sir Walter is a respected baronet, he has little money and cannot offer a sizeable dowry to attract a man for Anne. So had Wentworth not come back into her life, what would have become of her? She would have lived with Sir Walter and Elizabeth for as long as he lived, in that unfriendly house where she knew she was not wanted or loved. She could also stay with Lady Russell at Kellynch Lodge or with Mary at Uppercross—but she would have no comfortable home of her own, no real independence, as Austen would put it.

"One who had no distrust of herself"

Austen once again shows us the vulnerability of women in *Persuasion*—but she also shows us confident women who have learned what they want from life. One of Austen's achievements in the novel is her portrayal of the Admiral's wife Mrs. Croft, a capable person who is strong and adventurous:

Mrs. Croft, though neither tall nor fat, had a squareness, uprightness, and vigour of form, which gave importance to her person. She had bright dark eyes, good teeth, and altogether an agreeable face; though her reddened and weather-beaten complexion, the consequence of her having been almost as much at sea as her husband, made her seem to have lived some years longer in the world than her real eight and thirty. Her manners were open, easy, and decided, like one who had no distrust of herself, and no doubts of what to do; without any approach to coarseness, however, or any want of good humour.

Mrs. Croft also argues with her brother Captain Wentworth over his belief that women do not belong on a ship: "But I hate to hear you talking so, like a fine gentleman, and as if women were all fine ladies, instead of rational creatures. We none of us expect to be in smooth water all our days." Mrs. Croft then tells of crossing the Atlantic four times and other voyages, and concludes by saying that she has found her greatest happiness aboard a ship.

We see Anne become more willing to express herself as the novel progresses—she appears to gain some of Mrs. Croft's confidence. This is most obvious in chapter 11 when she contradicts Captain Harville, who declares that men are more constant in love than women. Anne argues that women are more loyal to their love. In response to this, Harville tells Anne

that "all histories are against you, all stories, prose and verse"—all prove, Harville claims, that women are

Austen's portrayals of women like Mrs. Croft and Anne suggest that in her future novels, had she lived past age forty-one, she may have focused on more mature women.

inconstant, to which he adds, "But perhaps you will say, these were all written by men." Which is exactly what Anne says:

> " 'Yes, yes, if you please, no reference to examples in books. Men have had every advantage of us in telling their own story. Education has been theirs in so much higher a degree; the pen has been in their hands. I will not allow books to prove any thing.' "

Looking over Jane Austen's Shoulder

WE GET TO SEE AN interesting element in *Persuasion* that we don't see in other of Jane Austen's novels: an editing decision. Austen wrote two chapter 10s—one that she cut, and the one that is included in the novel. The one that she discards is somewhat contrived: Captain Wentworth is convinced by his brother-in-law Admiral Croft to ask Anne whether the rumors that she will marry Mr. Elliot are true, and if so, will she and Mr. Elliot want to live in Kellynch-Hall again and end the Crofts' lease? When Anne assures Wentworth that she will not marry the Elliot heir, he admits his love, and they quickly reunite. Had Austen kept this chapter, the novel would have skipped the vital chapter 11, where Anne's eloquence on the subject of love and her observation about men's advantages make possible the lovers' reunion. But Austen knew better. As her nephew James Edward tells us, Austen did not like her first chapter 10: "Her performance did not satisfy her. She thought it tame and flat, and was desirous of producing something better." Austen was disappointed enough with the first draft that she became somewhat depressed about it. So she went to work again, writing two new chapters. Doing so gave her Anne a chance

to voice her frustration with being a woman in a culture where men get to see the world and are commissioned to write all histories, all stories, all prose and verse.

The Austen family held onto the cancelled chapter, and in the second edition of *Memoir of Jane Austen*, James Edward includes it. We appreciate this—but as usual with Austen's family, who went to such effort to portray their Jane as delicate and proper, James Edward labels the vital conversation between Captain Harville and Anne Elliot as merely "charming."

La lettre, painting by an unknown English artist circa 1843.

Her eloquence in this conversation about love, while Captain Wentworth is in the room, prompts him to speak at last and tell her how much he still cares. Austen's irony is also delicious here. Not allowing books to prove anything? Come now—Jane Austen's books prove a great deal.

Looking toward the future

Austen's portrayals of women like Mrs. Croft and Anne suggest that in her future novels, had she lived past age forty-one, she may have focused on more mature women; Anne is twenty-seven, unlike the younger women Austen had written of before (in all of Austen's other novels, her heroines are twenty or younger as the novel begins). Austen may have presented more heroines who argued openly with men and pointed out the unfair advantages that men have over women. She may also have intended to write of more women like Mrs. Croft and Anne, women who lived through challenging times but who became stronger as a result.

The famous writer of the early twentieth century Virginia Woolf found *Persuasion* particularly impressive, and notes the changes between the Jane Austen of the earlier novels and the Jane Austen of *Persuasion*. She looks carefully at scenes like the one in Bath when Wentworth goes in pursuit of Anne and she ignores her family and steps up to speak to him. Woolf also notes Austen's newfound bravery:

> *"There is an expressed emotion in the scene at the concert and in the famous talk about woman's constancy which proves not merely the biographical fact that Jane Austen had loved, but the aesthetic fact that she was no longer afraid to say so."*

As with her "questionable" moral that young people should choose their own partners in life, the scenes Woolf mentions show Austen as a bolder writer, expressing even deeper emotions and experiences than she had before.

Woolf also wonders about the "six novels that Jane Austen did not write"—what she might have produced if she had lived longer. She believes that Austen would have used dialogue less and reflections on the inner lives of her characters more, just as she does in *Persuasion*: "She would have devised a method, clear and composed as ever, but deeper and more suggestive, for conveying, not only what people say, but what they leave unsaid, not only what they are, but what life is." *Persuasion* does appear to be on such a trajectory.

Jane Austen's gift to Anne

Although Jane Austen herself had only just begun to taste freedom in her own writing, she gives Anne Elliot a wider freedom and hard-won happiness. The satisfaction and joy in this story of second chances comes through beautifully in the final scene of the

Although Jane Austen herself had only just begun to taste freedom in her own writing, she gives Anne Elliot a wider freedom.

BBC's fine 1995 adaptation of *Persuasion*. Anne is seen writing, sitting in the sun beside a window. She walks upstairs and outside into a beautiful day—she's on a ship, her husband's ship. She takes her place next to Captain Wentworth and they stand with the sun in their faces. The next shot is of the sunset as the heroine and hero sail off into it. With this last scene, we feel the depth of Austen's gift to Anne Elliot, the chance to heal a broken past and escape a dead-end life. It's an opportunity we wish we all had, to enjoy, finally, the sun upon our faces, and look forward to a better future—a future that, while standing next to a worthy lover, promises to be as fine and endless as the sea.

SELECTED BIBLIOGRAPHY

Armstrong, Nancy. *Desire and Domestic Fiction: A Political History of the Novel*. New York City: Oxford University Press, 1987. In this fascinating interpretation of the novel as a shaper of culture, Armstrong discusses Austen's involvement in the rise of the novel and the middle classes.

Austen, Jane. *The Works of Jane Austen*. Volumes I-VI edited by R.W. Chapman. London: Oxford University Press, 1923-1954. Generally considered the most reliable versions of Austen's novels.

Austen-Leigh, James Edward. *Memoir of Jane Austen*. London: Oxford University Press, 1926; first published 1870. This biography, written by Jane Austen's nephew, is invaluable.

Austen-Leigh, William and Richard Arthur Austen-Leigh. *Jane Austen: Her Life and Letters—A Family Record*. New York City: Russell & Russell, 1965. This useful biography of Austen by her great-nephew and great-great nephew, first published in 1913, presents more Austen family materials and memories of Jane Austen.

Butler, Marilyn. *Jane Austen and the War of Ideas*. London: Oxford University Press, 1975. Butler views Austen as essentially conservative in the context of the tumultuous time period in which she lived.

Butler, Marilyn. *Romantics, Rebels, and Reactionaries: English Literature and its Background 1760-1830*. New York City: Oxford University Press, 1981. Important history on the era that created Jane Austen.

Copeland, Edward and Juliet McMaster, eds. *The Cambridge Companion to Jane Austen*. New York City: Cambridge University Press, 1997. A useful collection of more recent essays on Jane Austen, including a handy timeline by Deirdre Le Faye.

Duckworth, Alistair. *The Improvement of the Estate: A Study of Jane Austen's Novels*. Baltimore: Johns Hopkins University Press, 1971. One of the influential interpretations of Austen as a conservative writer who was committed to traditional English culture and values.

Honan, Park. *Jane Austen: Her Life*. London: Weidenfeld & Nicolson, 1987. An excellent and carefully researched biography.

Kaplan, Deborah. *Jane Austen Among Women*. Baltimore: Johns Hopkins University Press, 1992. A compelling portrayal of Austen as being inspired and nurtured by a wide community of women.

Kirkham, Margaret. *Jane Austen, Feminism, and Fiction*. Totowa, NY: Barnes & Noble, 1983. A lively defense of Jane Austen as a quietly feminist writer.

Lambdin, Laura Cooner and Robert Thomas Lambdin. *A Companion to Jane Austen Studies*. Westport, CT: Greenwood Press, 2000. A collection of essays on Austen, including overviews of the critical response to each of her novels.

Le Faye, Deirdre. *Jane Austen: A Family Record*. New York City: Cambridge University Press, 1989. Another biography on Austen by a highly respected Austen scholar.

Le Faye, Deirdre, ed. *Jane Austen's Letters*. New York City: Oxford University Press, 1995. Austen's extant letters are vital in understanding her; this is a good place to start.

MacDonagh, Oliver. "Receiving and Spending: Sense and Sensibility," from *Jane Austen: An Anthology of Recent Criticism*. Edited by Harish Trivedi. Delhi: Pencraft International, 1996; pp. 112-138. A useful essay on the importance of money in Jane Austen's world.

Pool, Daniel. *What Jane Austen Ate and Charles Dickens Knew: From Fox Hunting to Whist—The Facts of Daily Life in Nineteenth-Century England*. New York City: Simon & Schuster, 1993. A quick way to get a glimpse of Austen's culture (and that of the Victorians).

Said, Edward. "Jane Austen and Empire: Mansfield Park," from *Jane Austen: An Anthology of Recent Criticism*. Edited by Harish Trivedi. Delhi: Pencraft International, 1996; pp. 150-169. This excerpted essay presents Said's central argument in regard to what he viewed as Austen's essential conservatism.

Southam, B.C., ed. *Jane Austen: The Critical Heritage*. New York City: Barnes & Noble, 1968. A collection of critical reviews written on Austen during her lifetime and through the first half of the nineteenth century.

Spense, Jon. *Becoming Jane Austen*. New York City: Hambledon Continuum, 2003. A readable if provocative biography on Jane Austen.

Stovel, Bruce and Lynn Weinlos Gregg. *The Talk in Jane Austen*. Edmonton, Alberta: University of Alberta Press, 2002. An interesting discussion of dialogue and language in Austen.

Todd, Janet. *The Cambridge Introduction to Jane Austen*. New York City: Cambridge University Press, 2006. Todd presents a good general history of Austen's life and times while arguing that Austen's great achievement was her creation of "psychologically believable and self-reflecting characters."

Tomalin, Claire. *Jane Austen: A Life*. New York City: Alfred A. Knopf, 1997. Another fine biography, with what may be the best guess at what Jane Austen's personality was really like.

Tyler, Natalie. *The Friendly Jane Austen*. New York City: Penguin, 1999. A fun and easy-to-read introduction to Jane Austen.

Watt, Ian, ed. *Jane Austen: A Collection of Critical Essays*. Englewood Cliffs, NJ: Prentice-Hall, 1963. A compilation of now classic critical essays on Jane Austen, including pieces by Virginia Woolf, Ian Watt, Lionel Trilling, Kingsley Amis, and D.W. Harding.

White, Gabrielle D.V. *Jane Austen in the Context of Abolition: 'a fling at the slave trade'*. New York City: Palgrave MacMillan, 2006. An intriguing portrayal of Austen's quiet support of the abolitionist movement.

ABOUT THE AUTHOR

Rebecca Dickson first encountered Jane Austen while in high school, when she was assigned to read *Pride and Prejudice*. She's been reading Austen's novels ever since. Jane Austen just might have inspired her to go on to college and eventually get a doctorate in English literature with a specialty in nineteenth-century writers. Though she shifted her focus to American authors, she is an avowed Anglophile and still a committed Austenite. She has published essays on Austen, Kate Chopin, and environmental issues, and she co-wrote with Frank Grady *Surviving the Day: An American POW in Japan*, an account of the POW experience in the Pacific during the Second World War. When not reading and writing about Jane Austen, she is hiking (she leads trips into the Colorado backcountry for the Sierra Club), biking, gardening, knitting, traveling, or visiting Brazil. She also loves cats and other animals and is a committed environmentalist. She teaches at the University of Colorado and lives in Boulder.

ACKNOWLEDGEMENTS

I'd like to thank my reading group—Karen Brock, Bev Daniels, Ron Flickinger, Traci Parker, and Audrey Zarr (also Jenna Rovegno, *in absentia*) for their inspiration over the last twelve years—their admiration of Jane Austen is matched only by their adoration of cheese, bread, chocolate, and wine. I'd also like to thank Steve Welter for his help with proofing and general support as I wrote the book. Deborah Viles and Christine Macdonald helped me decide on an approach that works while supporting my efforts—many thanks. Norlin Library at the University of Colorado at Boulder was essential—thank fortune for university libraries. And thanks also to the Jane Austen Society of North America; they have a handy Web site and are a collection of fine readers and writers. Two impressive biographers of Austen—Park Honan and Claire Tomalin—deserve recognition for their interpretations of her life, which I found invaluable. And thanks to Rachel Dickson for her inspired understanding of life and literature that has always been helpful to me, and for her observation that Jane Austen would consider us all dressed in merely our underwear. Thanks also to Frances Dickson, Jackie Jones, Stephanie Jones, Alletta House, Deirdre Butler, Peter Butler, Macon Cowles, Regina Cowles, Wendy Dubow, Sally Green, Gina Iannelli, Linda Nicita, Laura Wilson, and Amy Schlotthauer for their support while I was writing the book. And I'd like to acknowledge Dexter, Darcy, and Desdemona, who would have read Jane Austen if they could have, but instead they just curled up on my lap while I read her—they also kept me company while I wrote about her. Rest in peace, kitties.

Most importantly, I'd like to thank my editor Kjersti Egerdahl, who guided me through this project, contributed some fine ideas, and kept me on a tight but do-able schedule. Certainly this book could not have come into being without Kjersti and becker&mayer! Books. Thanks, Kjersti, for believing in this project.

For Steve and Rachel—and in memory of Ed Dickson

IMAGE CREDITS

Every effort has been made to trace copyright holders. If any unintended omissions have been made, becker&mayer! would be pleased to add appropriate acknowledgments in future editions.

Page 7: Library of Congress
Page 8: © 2008 Ron Flickinger Photography
Page 12: Jane Austen Memorial Trust
Page 13: Jane Austen Memorial Trust
Page 14: *The Sisters*, Usher, James W. (1845-1921) / Lincolnshire County Council, Usher Gallery, Lincoln, UK / The Bridgeman Art Library
Page 16: Chawton House and Church, 1809, English School (19th century) / Chawton House, Hampshire, UK / The Bridgeman Art Library
Page 18: Jane Austen Memorial Trust (all)
Page 23: The Gallery Collection / Corbis
Page 24: Hulton Archive / Getty Images
Page 27 (envelope): British Library (all)
Page 28: Stapleton Collection / Corbis
Page 30: *Young Woman on her Death Bed*, 1621 (oil on canvas), Flemish School (17th century) / Musee des Beaux-Arts, Rouen, France, Lauros / Giraudon / The Bridgeman Art Library
Page 33: *Signing the Register* (oil on canvas), Leighton, Edmund Blair (1853-1922) / © Bristol City Museum and Art Gallery, UK / The Bridgeman Art Library
Page 34: *The Waning Honeymoon*, 1878 (oil on canvas), Boughton, George Henry (1833-1905) / © Walters Art Museum, Baltimore, USA / The Bridgeman Art Library
Page 37: *Head and Shoulders of a Young Woman*, Greuze, Jean Baptiste (1725-1805) / Private Collection, Photo © Christie's Images / The Bridgeman Art Library
Page 38: Public domain image
Page 40: New York Public Library, The Carl H. Pforzheimer Collection of Shelley and His Circle
Page 41: *The Sisters*, 1839 (oil on canvas), Carpenter, Margaret Sarah (née Geddes) (1793-1872) / Victoria & Albert Museum, London, UK / The Bridgeman Art Library
Page 42: Courtesy of Chawton Village
Page 43: J. Butler-Kearney, Incorporated Photographer, Alton, Hants
Page 45: British Museum
Page 47: Public domain image
Page 49: *In the Depth of Winter*, Robinson, Frederick Cayley (1862-1927) / Private Collection / The Bridgeman Art Library
Page 50: Public domain image
Page 51 (envelope): The Granger Collection, New York
Page 52: "Offended two or three young ladies," the Bingley sisters from *Pride and Prejudice* by Jane Austen, 1894 (engraving) / Private Collection / The Bridgeman Art Library International

Page 55: "The Elevation of His Feelings," scene from *Pride and Prejudice* by Jane Austen (1775-1817) (engraving), English School (19th century) / Private Collection / The Bridgeman Art Library International
Page 57: Public domain image
Page 58: Public domain image
Page 60: Everett Collection / Rex USA
Page 64: Public domain image
Page 67: MGM / The Kobal Collection
Page 68: Stapleton Collection / Corbis
Page 70: Public domain image
Page 73: *Fanny and Jane Hamond*, Lawrence, Sir Thomas (1769-1830) / Private Collection, Photo © Bonhams, London, UK / The Bridgeman Art Library
Page 75: *At Her Desk*, Schafer, Henry Thomas (fl. 1873-1915) / Private Collection, © Mallett Gallery, London, UK / The Bridgeman Art Library
Page 77 (envelope): National Portrait Gallery, London
Page 79: Courtesy of Chawton Village
Page 81: Public domain image
Page 82: Public domain image
Page 85: Public domain image
Page 87: Joan Hassall
Page 88: Jane Austen Memorial Trust
Page 91: Joan Hassall
Page 92: Fanny Price at Mansfield Park with her cousin Edmund in the background, 1964 (gouache on paper), English School / Private Collection, © Look and Learn / The Bridgeman Art Library
Page 95: Corbis Sygma
Page 97: Corbis Sygma
Page 99: *Fanny Austen-Knight* (1793-1882) (watercolor on paper) by Cassandra Austen (c.1772-1845) / Private Collection/ The Bridgeman Art Library
Page 100: *The Prince Regent, later George IV (1762-1830) in his Garter Robes*, 1816 (oil on canvas), Lawrence, Sir Thomas (1769-1830) / Vatican Museums and Galleries, Vatican City, Italy, Giraudon / The Bridgeman Art Library
Page 101: AP Photo / Kinowelt
Page 103 (envelope): The Granger Collection, New York (all)
Page 105: Public domain image
Page 107: *The Harvest Field* (oil on canvas), Witherington, William Frederick (1785-1865) / Private Collection, Photo © Bonhams, London, UK / The Bridgeman Art Library
Page 108: *Godmersham Park, Kent, the Seat of Thomas Knight Esq.*, pub. in 1785 (engraving) (b/w photo), Watts, William (1752-1851) / Private Collection / The Bridgeman Art Library
Page 111: Public domain image
Page 112: Public domain image
Page 113: Stapleton Collection / Corbis
Page 115: Public domain image

Page 117: Public domain image
Page 118: Portrait of Charlotte Brontë (1816-55) (oil on canvas), Thompson, J.H. (19th century) / © Brontë Parsonage Museum, Haworth, Yorkshire, U.K. / The Bridgeman Art Library
Page 119: Public domain image
Page 121: *Faraway Thoughts*, West, Charles Cope (1811-90) / Private Collection, © Christopher Wood Gallery, London, UK / The Bridgeman Art Library
Page 123: *Orange Grove*, from *Bath Illustrated by a Series of Views*, engraved by John Hill (1770-1850) pub. by William Miller, 1805 (aquatint), Nattes, John Claude (c.1765-1822) (after) / Private Collection, The Stapleton Collection / The Bridgeman Art Library
Page 124: *Milsom Street*, from *Bath Illustrated by a Series of Views*, engraved by John Hill (1770-1850) pub. by William Miller, 1804 (aquatint), Nattes, John Claude (c.1765-1822) (after) / Private Collection, The Stapleton Collection / The Bridgeman Art Library
Page 125 (envelope): The Granger Collection, New York (letter); British Library (poem)
Page 126: Public domain image
Page 127: Public domain image
Page 129: Patrick Ward / CORBIS
Page 131: Public domain image
Page 132: *Young Orphan in the Cemetery*, 1824 (oil on canvas), Delacroix, (Ferdinand Victor) Eugene (1798-1863) / Louvre, Paris, France, Lauros / Giraudon / The Bridgeman Art Library
Page 135: Stan Honda / AFP / Getty Images
Page 137: *The Convalescent* (oil on canvas), Saintin, Jules Emile (1824-94) / © Bury Art Gallery and Museum, Lancashire, UK / The Bridgeman Art Library
Page 140: *Lordly Elevation*, pub. by Hannah Humphrey, 1802 (engraving), Gillray, James (1757-1815) / Private Collection, O'Shea Gallery, London, UK / The Bridgeman Art Library
Page 141 (envelope): Courtesy of the British Library (all)
Page 143: *The Naval Dockyard at Deptford*, Scott, Samuel (c.1702-72) / Morden College, Corporation of London, UK / The Bridgeman Art Library
Page 144: *View of a Country House*, c. 1840, English School (19th century) / Private Collection, © Gavin Graham Gallery, London, UK / The Bridgeman Art Library
Page 146: Stapleton Collection / Corbis
Page 149: Public domain image
Page 151: *Love Token* (oil on canvas), Frith, William Powell (1819-1909) / © Sheffield Galleries and Museums Trust, UK / The Bridgeman Art Library
Page 153: Public domain image
Page 154: *At the Pawnbroker's*, Lamont, Thomas Reynolds (1826-98) / Private Collection, © Christopher Wood Gallery, London, UK / The Bridgeman Art Library
Page 157: Abraham Solomon / Fine Art Photographic / Getty Images